The Valley of Baca (Weeping)

PUSH THROUGH THE NOISE & TEARS:

UNDERSTANDING, LOVE, FAITH, TRUTH & HEALING ARE ON THE OTHER SIDE

Allissen *C.* Jones

Let's Go to the Other Side Publishing

Let's Go to the Other Side Publishing
The Just Believe Project, Inc.
"Addressing the barriers to believing"
www.thevalleyofbaca.com
www.thejustbelieveproject.org

Photography by Evans Eye Photography Pasadena, California

<u>To my Creator, My Heavenly Father</u>

My Smile, My Joy, My Love…My Everything!

Your Love is remarkable, unmeasurable, and everlasting.

A Love that bulldozed through my walls to pick me up from my hiding closet.

With a mighty hand, you grabbed me just to cuddle me in your gentle arms.

You captured me.

Twirled me slowly… Round. Round and around in the mirror until I could see my true image.

Now awakened.

I live.

All of Heaven & Earth bellows your name. The trees worship as they dance in the air you have created. The mountains and hills stand in high honor of you While the grass bows in the breeze that gently whispers King of Kings.

The flowers and birds snap in rhythm of praise.

The oceans move their arms back and forth, back and forth, as their waving conveys your power.

The waves clap against the sand in defeat of ignorance as the hiss declares truth as freedom.

All of Earth is a reflection of your goodness and mercy.

I see you

Everywhere.

If I stubbornly make my bed in darkness you challenge me to
come out, if I chose to ascend the heights through
understanding thou art there.

Your love has taken me over and torn down the veil that
masked my heart, which attempted to keep us
Separated.

I am forever enamored.

You are the ink. Allow your word and truth to flow through
the bends and the circles of each letter. The tears found
between the sentences and the growth in the spaces between
my paragraphs are all to declare your Glory (your expressed
opinion).

I am your reflection.

One of your earthly expressions.

One of your finest creations.

I honor you, as the letters of my life unfold your goodness.

Power Realized and
Manifested.

My life exclaims, "Halle-Halle-lujah!"

The I AM, that I AM, that I AM!

I gladly smiled when you whispered in my ear,
"This one was born in
Zion"

Dedications:

Anthony D. Jones

To My husband, the very best friend I have ever known. Your dedication is relentless. You make it easy to be a wife and a mother. You keep me striving to bring out the best in me. I only want to give you my best.

Jihree D. Stewart, (God's provision)

At my lowest, I saw the pureness of your eyes and the beauty of your soul. A beauty so piercing, I had to get up.

Get up again. Get up again. Get up again. Get up Again.

Forever my first glimpse at Heaven.

An unselfish, unrelenting, and everlasting love.

I desire for the Spirit in my eyes to fuel the same resilience in your spirit.

Look at me.

Jelani Miles Jones (Mighty One)
There is not one day that goes by that you don't make me
laugh.
Your wit and heart is rare.
Your ability to believe in Mommy is encouraging
You are a huge part of the reason we are here
Jelani had 15 books sold when I was on chapter 3.
"Mommy, remember your gift to help people understand."
Daily as I was writing he would ask,
"Can you sign mine, yet?"
My little gentle encourager!
I love you!

To all my family.
Mom(s), Aunts, Cousins, Uncles, Brother and Sisters whom
allowed their worlds to stop to assist in mine. I will forever
appreciate your love and your fight.
Let's go to the Other Side.

Table of Contents:

Phase I: DECONSTRUCTION

And the fortress of the high fort of thy walls shall he bring down, lay low, and bring to the ground, even to the dust.

Ch.1 Strange land:
How can I sing your song in this Strange Land?

Ch.2 The Valley:
Multitudes, Multitudes, Multitudes in the Valley of decisions.
And go forth unto the valley, and proclaim the words that I tell thee,
And Isaac's servants digged in the valley, and found there a well of springing water

Phase II: ASCENSION
And he gave up the ghost and ascended into the heavens

Ch.3 Veils
Transforming
Spirit having an earthly experience

Ch.4 Vantage Point
How are you looking at your trial?
Calling versus declaring

Phase III: MANIFESTATION
He is waiting for manifestation of the sons of God

Ch.5 1 now see the God that sees me
You knew that? You recognize me?

Ch. 6 Let's Go to the Other Side
Mind Shift

Forward

For the last decade, I have voyaged through the darkness, the mysteries, the hills and labyrinths of the mind. I observe as a curious bystander as the spirit displays its entrapment to the panoply of our flesh. Our true nature agonizes as it rattles its chain to the enslavement of thought. Daily, in my career, I attempt to peel back the multiple layers of our enclosure. The epidermis, dermis, and then the subcutaneous layers of the skin are pealed slowly in order to free the spirit. The debridement process is painful; thus, creating extreme anxiety, trembles in speech, restless nights, and paralyzing fear. The gestures of deep, acute pain and uncontrollable emotions reveal layers of masked misunderstandings. The debridement is necessary to understand how our world appears; to reveal our snares and our motivations. The daily world of individuals I work with begin in the crevices of their minds.

Their thoughts take form in their outward world. As the mouth speaks I can identify problems, which enslave the spirit, as the agglomeration of skin unfold. Daily, I work with the real looking glass of individuals. The worldview they are unable to mask.

The real layers of skin are woven patterns
of pain, guilt, past mistakes, past joys,
misunderstandings, and redundant responses....

Studying behaviors and the power of the mind has
opened my eyes to the unbelievable power of thought.
Thoughts are restless and kinetic- they must and will create.
Picking apart the worldview of others by constantly searching
how they process information, their thoughts and understanding
of truth. I always find myself willfully and sometimes
reluctantly questioning my own understanding of truth and my
own contradictions in behavior. The very gentle nudge to
complete my writings after several years of journaling my
experience and my process of growth came from a much-
unexpected source.

Listen

It was a bright clear day in Southern California. I arrived in South Central, Los Angeles and I parked in front of my patient's home. I enjoyed mostly all aspects of my career and it is displayed in my interactions with my patients. I took some time to prepare myself before meeting with my patient, while sitting in my car. My morning began with the best and most important aspect of my day--prayer and meditation with God. My prayer, stillness and worship times begin at 3:00 a.m., daily.

During my workday, I continued to keep my mind on where I am and why God has me at this particular intersection. I carried my conversations with God, beyond our 3:00 a.m. prayer time by staying in a place of worship throughout my workday. William Murphy, Tasha Cobbs, William McDowell, Kim Walker, Kari Jobe…are constantly in rotation in my car as I travel within the inner city. Having revelation and knowing, he inhabits the praises of his people; I live in a place of worship and praise. When I am not in a situation to sing or speak of my praise. I want my life to demonstrate my highest praise.

On that beautiful morning, I made my way to my patient's door and he greets me hurriedly in his normal fashion; he unlocks the door quickly and takes five large steps away from the door. I slowly pushed the door open and look to the right, and my patient is already sitting at his kitchen table. His eyes moved in rapid motion as his heart paced.

I allowed some time for deep breaths as he relaxed from having to unlock his own front door. After allowing some time of rest....we began.

I endeavored to peel back more layers of his world by pulling at the ponderings in his mind. The swirls that have leaped from his perception has now made a haze throughout his home.

Reality is foggy.

Near the end of our meeting, his speech became very rapid and he began to fidget; he anticipates my nudge for him to walk with me outside on his own porch. He glanced at the clock and once again, his anxiety increases, knowing that moments in time would end our discussion.

Knowing the end of our meeting included a request for him to recreate his world by stepping through the fog and into the sun. Each step, his outward frame trembled as he displayed continued misunderstandings. I made a professional decision and we turned away from his door; his anxiety reached an intense level and his trembling uncontrollable. We returned to his comfort zone.

His breathing slowly returned to normal. He wiped the sweat off his forehead. "Wow, you almost made it close to your own front door;" I encouraged him for even attempting. His perception and understanding remained unchanged.

I observed him for a little while after and we simply talked.

During this time he makes mention of his 'attack'.

The patient is able to describe in detail a vicious attack perpetrated by a large group of men over twenty years prior. He describes walking to the local store, where he was approached by five men. The group of men began to tug and pull on him and the tugs progressed to violent hits and kicks. The patient does not miss a punch, a kick, a spat, nor a harsh word spoken by his attackers. He is able to describe the attack in very vivid details; he is able to recall the blood running down his face and the feel of the cold cement as he laid there wishing for the attack to be over. After working with this patient for a few years and hearing 'the attack' repeatedly. I am also able to describe 'the attack' in just as much detail.

On this particular day while at his home. I heard a loud shriek in the background as his mother nearly collapsed in my arms. She cried out, "I just want him to be normal! I just want him to be normal!"

The mother's skin was like a raisin and her eyes the color of an orange. I could see through her eyes, many layers of skin also ensnarled her spirit. The tears poured through her guilt-ridden view as she continued to scream,

"THE ATTACK NEVER HAPPENED, HE WAS NEVER ATTACKED!"

I explained to mom that the patient and the family unit would have to live within his new normal until he can progress. His mother continued to look at me and repeated, "The attack never happened! It is not real! The attack never happened! He was never attacked!"

I was floored and my first reaction was to calm her down. Mom, must be overwhelmed and saying the comments out of frustration. In my mind quickly I responded- "There is no way the attack never happened! No way! This man remains locked in his home, behind something that never happened! Literally, this man is a prisoner in this place!"

The confusion in the home continued as the patient became frustrated with his mother. I observed his reaction to his mother's comments and I noticed a pattern. The patient's response was one I had seen repeatedly in others, 'How can you tell me my delusions are delusions?' I quickly placed myself in the various viewpoints of this moment and I needed to quickly step out of the mist.

I stepped out of the confusion and into the fresh air. I shook my body vigorously in the sun to shake off the residue of their dead skin as I left their world. I immediately headed back to our clinic to discuss with doctors. To my dismay, in fact the attack never happened. I was flabbergasted!

I replayed our discussions repeatedly. I could not fathom I was dealing with a fixed delusion.

A delusion, a belief that is not amenable to change in light of conflicting evidence. I have worked with individuals with fixed delusions prior; however, this scenario was weighing in on me. Generally, there will be a hole in the story somewhere. Somewhere, I can notice the fallacy as the story repeats. However, not this time. The story did not change.

Truly, this fixed delusion was unaltered, consistent, and impossible to interrupt. I scratched my head as I considered how often he must meditate on this attack. Every second, every hour of every day in order for it to remain unaltered.

Days began to pass and I still could not shake my feeling… "Should I move him off my caseload?"

Throughout the day, I would find myself shaking my head in disbelief and I would sigh as I reflected on his case. Some days I would sit in my car and I would talk it out in my own monologue:

> "Twenty years this man has been locked in his home!
> He trembles!
> He shakes at the mention of going close to his own front door.
> He has had numerous suicide attempts based off this attack!
> The last suicide attempt was just weeks prior.
> He does not leave his home and trembles when I mention the sun or the cool breeze; reminders of being out of his comfort zone brings him to a breaking point.
> He has mentioned this attack from day one. Where

did I miss it?
If I can place myself in my patient's shoes, I can assist them with a way out.
Not this time! I do not understand this one or maybe, I don't want to understand."

After my monologue, something was tugging on me. I began to feel a nudge for me to go inward to seek why this particular case stayed with me. During my prayer time, I would push it away...

"Alright, Lord, I know this has something to do with my own life and for some reason, Lord, I am not ready for another skin shucking.
Praise music on and Kim Walker it is today!"

I turned it up loud. I found myself singing praise songs instead of welcoming the silence. I wanted to understand what was trying to communicate to me above this realm. However, I was resistant. Hours turned into days. Days turned into weeks; the mosquito by my ear would not leave me alone. During prayer time I still found myself over-singing Tasha Cobbs to drown out my inner voice. I was resisting the very answers to the questions I was asking. But why?

My self-honesty kicked in and I knew in some way this would require more debridement, more layers of my skin I needed to shave.

One morning while in my 3:00 a.m. time with God, I allowed praise, worship and the stillness/ inward process to begin. Once in the stillness-quickly a question, "What is a delusion?"

I smiled for that was easy to answer:

> "Alright God, Delusions are beliefs or impressions
> that are firmly maintained, despite being
> contradicted by the truth.
> My psychological education would define a
> delusion as a belief contrary to reality/truth,
> firmly held in spite of evidence to the contrary.
> A Delusion is an idiosyncratic belief or
> impression. Delusions are…."

As I began to talk it out my resistance crumbled, I curled inward more. I clearly heard—

"DELUSIONAL, HUMM NOT WALKING IN TRUTH. SOUNDS LIKE YOU HAVE THE TENDENCY TO DO THIS AS WELL!"

I squealed as if my legs were being waxed. Instantly, skin was yanked off. Next, I was bombarded with questions:

> "What keeps you trapped in the safety of your home?
> "What is keeping you in your comfort zone?"
> "What are you walking by? Truth? Or You?"
> "What happened to the book?"

I stuttered all my justifications:

"Lord, I-I-I- I know I am almost done with my doctorate and I will finish the book when I am a licensed Psychologist and then it will be perceived or received with more credibility. Fear has nothing to do with it, it just has to do with timing. God, you know I tell my story to anyone who is willing to listen and wants to hear, but, but, but...."

A gentle, however, correcting voice said,

"You may call his delusional; however, what would you call your resistance to walk in TRUTH?"

Ouch! That debridement of my flesh hurt! The pain was real; however, I needed to stay with it to understand the true source of the pain. I was frustrated with myself; I could see my truly awakening experience, which allowed me to see my identity according to truth.

The work it took to pull apart my worldview and perception over the last couple of years, including my ability to understand truth. Now several years out, I was sliding back into seeing things with my natural eyes. Going inward and receiving the correction; I began to call a thing a thing.

"Wow, God you are right and I missed it! Perceived fear, imminent fear, conditioned fear, passive and hidden fear are all the same and produce the same results."

With an unveiled heart I could see the similarities between my patient and I. For me to walk outside of spiritual laws/truths/understandings is a delusion (holding on to a belief despite superior evidence to the TRUTH). Having revelation and a shift from seeing with my natural eyes.

Having adopted spiritual truths as my necessary foundation. Truth declares we are made in his image and if I am conscious enough to accept my identity then there is no need for me to live under diminished ability.

"These words I speak unto you I speak not of myself; but of my father that dwelleth IN me, he doeth the works." I know you take no greater joy than to know we are walking in truth as the freedom and power that is evident of truth displays in our lives. After all my excuses, I honestly answered and the word delusion simply means a belief held with strong conviction, despite superior evidence to the contrary. I reminded myself;

> "Allissen, examine, test and evaluate yourself to see whether you are holding to your faith and showing the proper fruits of it. Realize and know through ever-increasing experiences that you are made in his image, in his image.. he made me."

After my time with some deep introspection the area that was once painful, now illuminated.

The tears flowed. I looked upon my reflection. I could see my own error in thought. My resistance to walk in my understanding of truth. In an act of understanding and true repentance (a mind shift), I compiled my writings and here we are…

Therefore, let us begin with a simple prayer and my heart's desire to run over into the life of someone else.

Simple Prayer

God, My Almighty father, the author and finisher of my story, whom I love dearly. I honor you with my life and my service to your people. God, use my life as an example of manifesting spiritual truths through the vestiges of flesh we continue to empower.

We are no longer blind to our misunderstandings and feel we are in your will, because we simply quote your word with no understanding...with no understanding.

We will not stop until we recognize we are a walking example of your love, power and image continuing to shine in this earthly realm; manifesting spiritual truths at various levels of test and trials.

Passing from lower levels of understanding to spiritual enlightenment (the ability to see our lives in totality). God, we are preparing our minds for action. God, let my life reflect how to hunger after understanding and attain wisdom in the face of any adversity.

Recognizing the essential fact that we are spiritual beings having an earthly experience.

We were indeed made in your image; in the image of God, we were created.

God Almighty, my King, and my Heavenly Father, thank you that our strength will forever be in you.

God touch the heart of the reader.

Help the veils that still cover our hearts to be removed and their eyes opened to see my story on a spiritual level, (to grasp meaning to apply to their physical world).

Allow the reader to see any obstacle they may be currently in, as something that is passable. Allow my story to become alive to the reader to see hope and not despair. Belief and not doubt. Love and not condemnation. To that ole' adversary, whom speaks of darkness, lies, and misunderstandings all we do is speak the truth.

Today we respond to any hindrances, any accusations that would attempt to exalt itself against the knowledge of God. We simply say,

"It is written, you shall worship, the Lord your God, and Him only shall you serve. AWAY WITH YOU!"

That is the only mention of the adversary we will give and the rest of our concentrations will remain on going inward to build up our knowledge and understanding of truth in order to tear down the barriers we have created within ourselves that keep us from seeing more manifestation.

Lord Jesus Christ, where I have missed it, I repent.

Now, expose those areas that caused me to miss it, therefore, allowing real understanding and a real mind shift (repentance) as we grow from strength to strength in you.

Amen.

Psalms 84; 5-7

"Blessed are those whose strength is in you,

Who have set their hearts on pilgrimage.

As they pass through the Valley of Baca,

They make it a place of springs;

The autumn rain cover it with pools.

They go from strength to strength

Till each appears before God in Zion."

My request:

Now open your minds, allow a close look inward as we pass through the phases of looking at a challenge.

Pay attention to the process-- not just the outcome.

God already knows all; therefore, be honest with you, no matter how painful it may become.

Let us process the pain and truly learn how to move from strength to strength through the application of truth.

Ask questions when you are reading & then make those questions personal regarding your situation.

Turn the questions inward. Turn the questions inward. Turn the questions inward.

Take notes

Remain open-minded.

"Do not believe me unless I do what my Father does. But if I do it, even though you do not believe the miracles, which you may know and understand that the Father is in me, and I in the Father. John 10:37

Deconstruction Phase:

THE CONSCIOUS DISSECTION OF AN
UNDERSTANDING OR BELIEF,
TO THE POINT OF EXPOSING THE
CONTRADICTIONS IN BEHAVIOR AND
INTERNAL OPPOSITIONS WHICH KEEP THE
VERY BELIEF FROM MANIFESTATION.
Allissen C. Jones

What do you believe?
Do you understand what you believe?
Does your behavior line-up with what you believe?

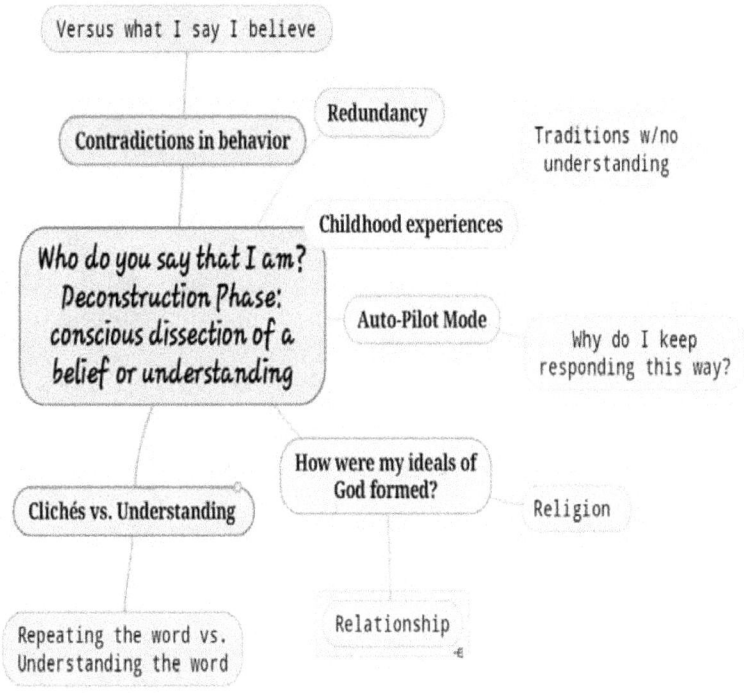

Versus what I say I believe

Contradictions in behavior

Redundancy

Traditions w/no understanding

Childhood experiences

Who do you say that I am? Deconstruction Phase: conscious dissection of a belief or understanding

Auto-Pilot Mode

Why do I keep responding this way?

Clichés vs. Understanding

How were my ideals of God formed?

Religion

Repeating the word vs. Understanding the word

Relationship

Strange land

The fall of 2006 felt like an Indian summer.

All of the normal seasonal changes were present as red and brown leaves began to cover the grass. All of our summer time attire packed away and light sweaters pulled out in preparation for the change in weather. School buses were back in rotation and crossing guards back at their post. For it to be fall, the weather still felt abnormally dry. California desert weather normally averaged 90-105 degrees during the summer; however, generally the cooler winds would swirl in around October. I can recall seeing my son's thin jacket hanging on the wall rack instead of the heavier jacket generally needed around this time of year. In the heat of the day, my wood floors would assist with keeping the house a little cooler allowing me some pleasure to just simply slide off from my couch and extend my arms and legs on the cold floor. In the coolness, I would sit and reflect on the several task staring at me eye to eye.

As I enjoyed the coolness and quietness of the moment, my son entered the room, snuggled right under my arms and laid parallel to my body. Inwardly and outwardly I began to smile. My smile encompassed multiple meanings. Internally, I enjoyed his warm touch and the embrace of his unconditional love. While on the other hand, my smile was more reflective of a laugh and the sacrificial love of a mother.

As I enjoyed the tranquility and the necessity of allowing my thoughts to flow freely in this space of time to assist me with preparing for my daunting week; a gust of musty body heat disturbed my pondering and coolness.

Although we sat in complete silence as his sweaty body heat swirled around the room further masking the coolness. We both remained silent for neither one of us needed to say a word, for our minds were busy with chatter.

We laid there still in our own experiences; however, allowed everything else to shut down in order to live in the closeness of this moment.

After enough silence and recharging, "Mom, what are we having for dinner?" uhh... I knew this meant my quiet time was not only interrupted... it was over. Having accepted my role as a single mother, rejuvenation came in the form of short exhales, quick naps and long hot baths. With my quiet moment now over, the mundane duties of our home where now calling me: the dishes, groceries, vacuuming, the laundry, the mortgage, the gardener, the utilities, my home business all began to call my name in a very demanding and unrelenting voice, "Allissen, we all need you!"

At this point, my life-resembled moments of peace and quiet with lots of hard work. My life was comprised of long days and nights; however, with all the hastiness, my life felt right.

Before we sat down for Sunday dinner, several of my weekly tasks were completed. My home smelled of lemongrass and gardenia; my oak wood floors shined and my kitchen sparkled. My work clothes for the week prepared; his school clothes and football uniforms all pressed. I twirled around with an internal sense of accomplishment and joyfully blurted, "It is finished!" I continued to laugh while I murmured,

"It is finished...for today or until he walks in my room, and needed something else."

My days as a single mother were often hectic and my list of things to do would range from breakfast, making sure we both had clean clothing, lunches, and getting out of the house on-time without leaving my house a mess. I enjoyed returning from a long day to a neat and organized home; Order and organization at least helped me keep all my affairs running somewhat smoothly.

During my drive to work, I often found myself recalling all the bills I paid, needed to pay and even the ones that would just have to wait.

There was never a dull moment and I forced myself to make some of the moments quiet. At this time, I was close to twenty-eight years of age.

I was very happy and comfortable in the last three years after my divorce. Living happily single, my income tripled and I was making well over six-figures. By age twenty-eight I was very near two-hundred thousand per year; I realized the harder I worked the more since of security it would bring. Happily divorced, I stayed in the mindset of doing whatever I needed to do for my son and I to be well. Each day, I did what I needed to do.

My days were long and stressful. This was my life. Day in and day out.

On one particular night after a busy day the sun was set and the half-moon was rising to its peak. The temperatures slowly started to cool, allowing me the pleasure of opening my large five windows in my room. A cooler and gentle breeze brushed the whispering wind through my windows nudging the lemongrass and gardenia scents throughout our home. I loved the comforts of my home. Even when it felt like a third or fourth job.

"Did you brush your teeth, Jih?"

"Yes, mom," he replied, as we fell to our knees on the side of his bed. I chose not to make his half-brushed teeth a battle at this point in our night. His homework was complete. He ate a somewhat balanced meal and he washed the funk off. We closed our eyes and locked our hands in agreement, fell to our knees and we began:

"Our Father which art in heaven, Hallowed be thy name. Thy kingdom come. Thy will be done in earth, as it is in heaven.
Give us this day our daily bread.

And forgive us our debts, as we forgive our debtors. And lead us not into temptation, but deliver us from evil: For thine is the kingdom, and the power, and the glory, forever. Amen"

After repeating the Lord's Prayer, Jihree began to say his personal prayer for his parents, cousins, grandparents, friends, teachers, pets....We concluded our prayer with, "thank you for giving us wisdom and understanding. Amen."

I smacked a kiss on his Hershey colored skin and rolled his blankets over his chest; I turned to exit his room and looked back at him one last time before my index finger turned down his light switch. The light in his room slowly went dark and my feet began to tap dance. The dimness in his room and the silence from his mouth created a conditioned response for me to beam and moonwalk all the way to my room. It was now my alone time.

My rejuvenation time began with a plethora of candles: small ones, tall ones, wide ones, round ones, and fragranced ones. Lights were unnecessary in my room, nor the bathroom for my small candle show lit up both areas. My room was large and open, with my large cherry wood pillar bed stationed in the center.

My favorite bed sat in the middle of my attempt at tranquility. There were five large uncovered windows, which created a freedom I enjoyed. My large bed was cozy and I enjoyed sleeping in it alone. I sniffed my sheets and pillows while waiting on my bath water. Oh' how I enjoyed the simple pleasures of sliding into my bed after soaking.

The water was ready and hot. Lights out and windows opened. The air was freely able to flow in at this point, tickling the outer layers of my butter pecan skin. The calmness of the water and the flickering of the candles forced all other thoughts to standstill.

The dim light from the candle stems combined with the tantalizing heat from the water kept me completely engaged. My mind completely captured; I was able to keep my thoughts right on the heat, candles and water; no bills, no needs, and no one calling my name. After immersion in my version of tranquility for a portion of time, the breeze from my windows altered the heat of my water turning it to a chilly cold. That was my queue; time to get out. My bed was waiting on me as my sheets called my name.

I slid into my bed and grabbed my remote. "SUV: Law & Order time!" Somewhere on some channel it was always on. The time was 11:00 p.m. I hushed my inner-thoughts that counted down the hours before my next work day. I needed to be up by 5:00 a.m., but I laid there on my soft sheets still enjoying my 'me -time.' In some weird way I knew as soon as I closed my eyes my 'me time' would end. My alarm would be the next sound I heard triggering my daily race.

As much as I resisted sleep my body had a way of winning. I would make it to the point of Olivia and Elliot catching the perp; however, I always missed the judicial process. My eyes slowly succumbed to the light weights placed on each eyelid. My body would melt into the coolness of my blankets and sheets as I slowly entered sleep.

After several slaps to my alarm clock, my morning began. I often wondered how it still functioned after much abuse. After an extra five minutes in bed I knew I would be creating greater opposition if I did not fight the weights on my eyes and my body's inability to leave the softness of my sheets. "Get up, Allissen!"

Monday in my view appeared like a gateway to the beginning of a long week filled with monotonous hours of me looking like a professional clown at a circus. I juggled task with two hands, my mouth, my feet, and a few bounced off my head.

I opened my eyes. I hit the floor with my to-do-list on my mind and an ice-cold Coke in my hand. "Let's make this week count." Once up and moving around some parts of my day felt automatic.

The activities took very little thought and through redundancy I did not have to be very conscious of the activities. My house alarm, kid and his backpack, my purse and of course the kid we all made it into my silver Range Rover and rolled out of the garage and down the driveway. '*Victory*,' by Ty Tribbet blared through my speakers and got us moving in the car and once again, we grabbed hands in agreement and prayed.

"Thank you for a new morning and a new day; cover my son with your blood and keep us both safe from harm and danger. Amen."

Jihree, made it to school on time and I made it to work. "Thank you, Jesus!"

My workday began with working side by side with the owner of a commercial real estate company. We discussed current deals, marketing ideas, hiring needs, and all the dealings that pertained to keeping the company running.

My Lunch breaks included the local fast food drive-thru and of course my Coke to get me through the remainder of my day. As the time neared 4:00 p.m., my mind and body would once again shift to autopilot mode. "Closing time! Bye Kevin, same place, same time, but different day."

During my ride home I would return calls to my own real estate clients. I mentally prepared another keep-me-busy list for the work I needed to complete once I reached my home office.

Once home, residential deals and finance deals would consume the next several hours of my day. On that particular day I needed to make a quick stop at a local escrow company. There was always a smile on my face and a sense of accomplishment when I reached this stage of a transaction. "Hey Allissen, you are here again this week, you are doing it," said my escrow representative. I signed where I needed to sign; I grabbed my check and smiled while I danced the two-step all the way to my car.

In some way all the hard work felt easier when I held a very large commission check in my hand. Flashbacks of working and never having enough always crossed my mind. I desired never to return to that place of uncertainty. Therefore, I drove home to start my second job.

Once again, on this night, like most other nights I stretched my 'me-time' as long as possible before my eyes defeated my will.

One Friday afternoon in October, the weather began to change and the heat was not so draining. Actually on this Friday once we arrived home, I remember standing in my driveway and looking up at the sky. As I looked up at the sky, I could smell a storm. The greyish color of the clouds and their stacked formation told me something was brewing.

"Something is rolling in our way and we are about to have an interruption in our sunny days."

I stared intently at the clouds for I could see something was coming; however, with my natural eyes I could not measure the magnitude of the storm. A little rain would be welcomed; however, I sighed at the thought of a full on storm. Subtly, I knew I was unprepared and heavy rain would cause my commonplace activities to become further demanding.

Once inside my home and into my routine I shut my windows tight to avoid having too much wind and cold effect the warmth inside my home.

I looked at Jih' and in my Hammer-time voice shouted, "Heater time!"

In some way Jih' was able to perceive a change was coming and he lovingly asked, "Can I sleep with you tonight?" I replied reluctantly, "sure" I sighed after agreeing for I knowingly gave up my rejuvenation time. In order for him to sleep my television remained off. "No Law & Order tonight." We locked hands in agreement as we began our nightly prayer; "Our father which art in heaven, hallowed be thy name...." At the conclusion of our prayer, Jihree looked through me with great perplexity,

"Mom, why do we say this prayer every night?"
His question was thought provoking and it forced a paused in our automatic mode. Searching the crevices of my own understanding left me questioning my motherhood and my own level of understanding. Several questions began to flood my

mind once my autopilot mode was interrupted;

"Am I not teaching him about God correctly?

Why do I say this prayer with him, humm without teaching him understanding? Where and why did I learn this prayer?"

I closed my eyes and thought back to my own youth.

My daily prayers with my mother and brother included this prayer and this was the prayer we were taught.

Looking into my son's large eyes, I gave him my truth.

"Jih', we say this prayer nightly because my mom said it with me."

Through the wrinkles in his forehead and his raised eyebrows, I could see my answer did not satisfy his thirst for understanding. I kissed his raised brows and redirected the conversation by using my stern voice, "time to close your eyes!"

A heavy silence filled the room; I was accustomed to falling asleep to the Law & Order chimes. The peculiar silence caused me to fall asleep very rapidly and into a deep sleep. The sleep felt very restful. I did not count the hours of sleep I would have before the gunshot triggering my race would sound off. I tried to keep the thoughts of my alarm out of my mind.

Forgetting what was coming on the next day, I let go of my resistance and willingly closed my eyes for sleep.

My sleep was restful, as my mind lazily drifted in stillness.

Slowly from rest I opened my eyes to an ominous light. My eyes squinted in the light as I struggled to use my hand as a shield from the brightness. I slowly looked around and my room felt very unfamiliar. The colors were a dull blue and the room felt dim and heavy. The openness, tranquility and freedom was absent from my room. My large five windows were masked by concrete.

Somehow, I was closed-in. Trapped, and unable to freely move. The softness of my familiar sheets was absent, in their place was a lump mattress and dry white sheet. Finally, a familiar face as I turned left, "Jihree," my crackly voice was dry. "What are you doing next to my bed?" I vaguely remembered him in my bed when we went to sleep. He replied with a smile, "Get some rest."

My mouth twisted in confusion for I could not understand the slight tears drizzling from his eyes. I leaned further on my side to gage what was going on with my son. I lifted my arm to wipe his tears with the outer portion of my hand. I moved my arm and a piercing pain shot from my arm then down into my spine. Suddenly, a large group of people entered the room all at the same time and interrupted me. The group dressed in white and blues carried large metal charts in their hands. The group made no sound, spoke no words. They touched me and the things around my bed simultaneously and never spoke a word.

My anger rolled from my belly as the invasion of my space

continued without my permission. My 'O-Hell-Naw' attitude could be seen in my eyes as someone gently nudged my son from my view. My focal point in all the confusion was moved; I could not find him.

A man with a white mask on grabbed my wrist, while another read from a chart near my feet. Two nurses stood near an I.V. running into the same arm where I felt the piercing pain. My eyes wide open and in a subtle form of shock. I was frozen to this unfamiliar bed; I struggled to gain their attention.

My opened mouth made no sound, as my brain stood challenged to make sense of all the hurrying about taking place all around me. My head weighed a ton, with every ounce of energy I possessed I leaned forward to look for my familiarity. I could not find him. The room moved in slow motion; my heartbeat bounced through my chest wall.

My thoughts raced in an effort to be faster than the previous dreadful thought moving swiftly through my mind. I was overwhelmed as fear and confusion nestled on my chest and legs. I struggled to push through the greyish/blueish walls, the people poking and prodding and the stuffiness of the suffocating room. Finally, my anger increased to a level which allowed to me to turn my emotions into energy. The energy passed by my vocal chords causing vibrations as I screamed, "JIHREE!"

Once my force released I was able to sit up. I turned to my

right and there were my five large windows. I touched my arms and no signs of I. V's. Frantically, I looked down and my 1,000 count sheets were still in place. I hopped up and stood over my bed. Jihree was soundly asleep. "Wow, that was a dream? It felt so real!"

I made it to my bathroom, I looked into the mirror and all was well. I turned back to my bed and my clock with red lights glowed bright 3:10 a.m. Humm... the time on the clock felt unsettling to me and the dream felt all too real. I sat in the center of my bed to process my dream. "What was that all about?" I pondered on the dream as long as I could until the heaviness of my eyes, the familiarity of my bed and the wee hours of the night won. I reluctantly fell back into a deep sleep.

The next several days it was very difficult for me to release my dream. After trenchant analysis, I connected my dream to a recent movie I watched on several occasions, _Wit._ I generally would play the DVD when I needed an excuse to let down my walls and cry like a big baby. I found myself watching the movie several times and felt at some subconscious level the movie was manifesting in my dream. Throughout the movie, The Holy Sonnet, by John Donne, repeated religiously:

"Death be not proud all though some have called thee
Mighty and dreadful, for thou are not so;
For those whom thou think'st thou dost overthrow
Die not, poor Death, nor yet canst thou kill me.

One short sleep past, we wake eternally,

And death shall be no more; Death thou shalt die." (John Donne, Holy Sonnets/1663)

The next morning, I decided to discuss my dream with a dear friend of mine.

"Anthony! Man, you know I had the weirdest dream last night! It felt undeniably real! I was sleep and then I wasn't. But I was in a hospital bed, I think… then I wasn't. I was able to wake myself up and guess what time it was…3:00 a.m.?"

Our dream discussion turned into an hour-long conversation with each other passing the mic to rant about various memorable dreams.

"Pass the mic back! Anthony, we are trying to figure out my dream, not the one where you are locked in a trunk somewhere or stuck in the middle of the ocean."

We laughed and my uncomfortableness with my dream eased as laughter filled the conversation shared between two garrulous friends.

"Allissen, you probably watched some of those crazy shows. I know you watched Ghost of Atlanta, Paranormal of Compton, or Spirit in the Refrigerator last night…say you didn't."

"Ha-Ha! Real funny, Mr. Jones," I replied.

Anthony knew how to make me laugh. After our conversation, the perplexity of my dream was now simplified.

"All right, all right no more _Wit._"

A few days passed with no dreams. My thoughts and questions of my vivid dream that eerily felt real still did not diminish. I continued my daily patterns. I kept on with business as usual.

Being very analytical, I dissected my thoughts, behaviors and dreams pretty consistently and for some reason this dream stayed in front of me like a highlighted note. Waiting on me to notice the color amongst the other patterns.

"But what? But Why?"

The interruption and over analysis caused a sap in my daily routine; bids to understand my dream flat out acquired entirely too much out of my already extended days. I happily and willfully accepted any resolve for my dilemma. I continued to push it away and eventually loaned out my '_Wit_' DVD.

"Amen, Bishop!" shouted the woman in the large hat. Church on Sunday took me to Gardena, California to the City of Refuge. The drive was a good two-hours for me; driving allotted time for more planning and more thoughts to run free. I used my time driving to church to plan my next moves. Praise music on all the way there; I was fully prepared for service once I arrived.

Clap…Clap…Clap…Shout!

"In the distance there is a light and I can see it shining bright; O' what joy we feel, it's a city to on a hill…
Come on let's go, we welcome you to the City of Refuge."

Beautiful music, I could vast in the sounds, words, and beats of the harmonious sounds. From time to time, I could stay in the beauty of a great song forever. Praise and Worship, the choir, the choir and the choir again; did not bother me. The music. Oh, the music; Psalms of David and the City of Refuge choir with their heavenly sounds forced me to extend my arms, stand to my feet and clap my hands. The melodious place created an energy, a life force.

Bishop Jones used his understanding of the mind and behavior in order to teach people how to apply scripture. How to live it. The message would make me: cry, repent, attempt to be better, walk in love and seek God's face until about Tuesday. Wednesday was a different story, "Bible study tonight in Los

Angeles. I cannot make it tonight, Lord." Wednesday Night
Bible Study was not happening; I drove a good two hours to get
there (each way) on Sunday. I was not driving again on
Wednesday. My conversation to God on Wednesday:

> "Lord, you know I have to be at work on Thursday
> morning and the kid has school. How about I just spend
> some time in your word on Wednesday night?"

I believed my bargaining was sufficient and once again, I
continued in what I knew.

The moments which encompassed time rolled on.
My daily life continued and I avoided any questioning of my
behavior, work schedules or sleep schedules. As the pilot, I
allowed our life to cruise as much as possible. Turbulence was
avoided or quickly rectified.

Cooler weather, shorter sunlit days and Halloween rolled by
without any blinks in my routine. Thanksgiving and Christmas
arrived with the usual weather, very little rain but colder days.

To my surprise, the middle of winter brought in an unusual
amount of rain; the rain poured down from the heavens
relentlessly. Yes, we needed rain; however, it came with its
share of gloom and inconvenience. Driving on the roads took
forever, making my days even longer. Traffic was slow and
accidents were plentiful. "Oh' no one can drive; it's just rain
people!"

On one particular rainy night after making it home to my place of warmth, peace and comfort. I touched a few of my files slightly and then decided they would have to wait. I decided to call it a night very early. After my required daily activities were completed, I turned the lights, television, radio, and phone off in anticipation of a great restful night of sleep. I bounced on my bed, felt the comfort of my sheets and closed my eyes voluntarily, no weights needed. The sleep was rejuvenating. The next morning, I felt as if I overslept.

The room was hazy. My thoughts felt foggy.

I was not quite ready to awake. During my attempt to gain focus, once again there was a piercing pain in my arm. I turned to my right and there was a nurse near my head,

"Allissen, time for chemo!" I smiled in agreement. I knew what was coming. Once up as far as my own energy could support me in the bed; somehow, I could see myself.

There were no mirrors... I could see myself.

The person I was able to glace upon, I did not recognize. I was bald, my skin pale and dry. I was very thin. My lips cracked from the piles of chapped skin. My licks were unable to soothe my dryness. Tears filled my eyes as confusion wrestled in my ears.

The tears did not stop any movement around me, for no one paid any attention to my tears.

My heartbeat visible through my throat. Anxiety caused me to panic. My breath became shallow. I barreled my chest out and in--out and in. Paralyzing fear.

I forced myself to breathe, by extending my chest to take in as much air as possible.

Straightaway, the sound of glass shattering all around me caused my stomach to drop. The calamity caused me to sit straight up. I sat up in the darkness and looked to my right and my large five windows were present. I looked down and my sheets, my duvet were there, no nurses in the room and no I.V.'s in my arm. I blinked my eyes several times in an effort to see in the darkness. My room felt very uncomfortable.

Beyond the touch, sight, sound and smell of my familiarity…something, did not sit well with my taste.

In my place of tranquility, the savor was tense and grim. I managed to look down on my floor and my large sixty- inch television was on the floor. I sought to wrap my mind around what I was seeing with my natural eyes with what I was sensing.

"How is this possible? This T.V. is too heavy."

I asked myself aloud as I realized, "It is not possible." Quickly a flood of thoughts stammered in as I wrapped my mind around the fact that this was impossible without physical force. I tussled with my options.

"1. RUN out of the house as quickly as possible or 2. Find your GUN."

I could not run out without the kid and he slept like a log, so that was not going to work.

"Where did my brother place the key to the gun case he purchased for me weeks prior? Shucks! Great, move Allissen, have a gun and not know how to get to it!!! You little Brainiac."

I slowly dangled my legs on the side of my bed as my eyes drifted to the only light in the room. The only light visible in the darkness glowed in red. My clock flashed in bright red numbers 3:03 a.m. 3:03 a.m. 3:03 a.m.

My mind churned in the worst possible storm. The heaviness in the room was not my own. I looked around with my natural eyes and nothing was visible. I grabbed the first object I could feel in the darkness. A-ha! My Coach 3-inch pump was still near my bed. "Yes, I knew you would come in handy one day." I walked slowly through my room with the heel pointing up. My plan was to aim for the eyes; in the natural, that shoe was my weapon. I made two leaps, like Olivia would in Law & Order. I hit my light switch and instantly my room was full of light.

Everything looked in place except, for the television on the floor; no intruder could be seen with my natural eyes. "Wow, something is here and I can feel it," I blurted anxiously.

Something beyond my visual eyes tapped into my spiritual senses. I could not shake the vibrations I felt, nor the smell that was near. The smell was not putrid or harsh; nevertheless, it just was not my own, nor the scent of my home.
The scent was like a gathering of flowers.

I was accustomed to living alone. I generally only slept with a porch light on. My house was completely pitch black.

Eventually, I gathered up enough courage to walk outside my room. I tiptoed down my hallway and made it to the first light switch. I turned the light on and looked around upstairs and there was nothing. There was nothing.
Everything was in place.

My son's room and the extra rooms were all in order. I headed downstairs; however, every light available to me was on at that point. The hallway lights, the recessed lighting on the stairs, the theater room lights, and all bedroom lights were on. The house on the corner was as bright as I could get it with man-made lights. I walked downstairs and everything was fine.

I looked up at my room door from my downstairs point of view, as I reluctantly climbed each stair.
Each step up each stair, I was unable to shake the feeling of another presence. I would walk three steps and then turn my head quickly to look behind me.

Something around me felt peculiar. My surroundings were uncharacteristic of the norm; awkwardly, at the same time something felt familiar. Each step I took I found myself looking back expecting to see someone.

Puzzled and exhausted by the time I reached my room. I laughed for ALL my lights would remain on that night.

I lifted my large big screen television, which remained screen down on my floor and placed it back in the correct position. The television fell with great force. I was amazed to see that it was in its original state and continued to function.

Overwhelming perplexity was now my pillow as I sat straight up in the middle of my bed. Sitting straight up gave me a 360-degree view of my room. I slowly glance to my right and there was that darn clock again; 3:10 a.m.

"WHAT? HECK No! The Devil is a Liar!"

My arsenal of scary movies played on repeat. I knew something was trying to communicate to me; but what?

I began to pray at full volume, and with great intensity. I called on the blood of Jesus and pulled out all the quoted scriptures I could recall. I walked through the house pleading the blood of Jesus, hollering, "No weapon formed against me shall prosper!" I shouted the few other scriptures I thought were fitting for this circumstance. Somewhat believing what I was saying; however, not necessarily knowing why or how to manifest the power in the words.

After I finished my verbal battling, in which I rebuked Satan, pleaded the blood of Jesus and called on a whole slew of angels in my battle. A sister was tired.

I spent a good, hard and long thirty minutes and wore myself out saying and doing things I had seen done before me in the time of need.

Once I felt Jesus, Mary, Moses, and host of angels had to hear me, I laid it on down.

My eyelids fluttered a few times to every sound heard in my home. Ever creek forced one eye to open. After a few more looks around the room and no one jumped out. The next sound I heard were the croaks of my alarm clock.

The sun was bright and my eyes sat on bags; I laughed for I still held on to my Coach heel as a weapon.

Daybreak came and I was back in my routine and everything felt normal. I said an additional prayer and determined I needed to abstain from television. I continued to cast down my thoughts thinking the basis of my dreams were from something I watched or ate.

I rationalized my experience and concluded the messages were for someone else. I set myself on a mission to figure out whom the messages were pertaining too.

Reflecting back now, I remember calling Anthony and telling him that he needed to go see a doctor. I even went as far as calling his doctor and making him an appointment. Anthony returned with a diagnosis of hypertension and I was pleased that I pushed him to see a doctor.

In my mind, the mystery was now solved.

Now, let us go on with life.

There was no further need to search the truth or truly process my dreams. I already figured it out. "Boom! Thank you Jesus!"

Eventually, the dreams stopped and the strange but familiar occurrences in my home ceased. I continued with my life as normal. Two jobs. My son. My home business. My Sunday church attendance and my Anthony.

In that space of time, I was happily single and I really did not have a desire to be married any time soon or ever, ever...ever. My official divorce from my first husband (my son's father) was coming up on four years now. I was happily in the swing of being a single mom again, legally.

Spiritually, I consistently attended the City of Refuge with Noel Jones on Sunday. I prayed daily consistently (what I called consistent), before we drove, before we ate and before we went to bed. My study routine included opening my bible and wherever the page landed,

"Lord that must be what you want me to study today! I knew all the common scriptures most of us pull out in the time of need; however, at that point in my life all was well. I paid my tithes and offerings and continued to love and take care of my son.

I spent my occasional adult time with a very close male friend and confidant when we were able to make time. However, at this point in my life, my focus was on my career and financial security.

My previous marriage was a true learning experience, in which I learned all I needed to learn in six months, after six months he was released to go teach someone else. We would make several attempts to reconcile, but I gladly accepted, "I am not the one for you. God, has someone for you, but I am not her!"

I decided to work on me to avoid some of my previous choices.

Marriage was far away from my plan; nevertheless, I knew I absolutely loved my friend and our friendship. During that time, I was twenty-nine, and Anthony was thirty-one; we both learned how to be great friends to one another during the last six years. He was genuine; I loved his heart for youth. I admired that he was a young African-American male who like me, grew up in the era of crack, gangs, and crime in the heart of Los Angeles and Compton, California.

Through the challenging environment, he still managed to achieve his Master's degree in Education.

I recognized there was something in him that would add value not only my life, but also to the life of my son and maybe a future little one. Recognizing quality and longevity in our relationship; nevertheless, we did not want to rush anything. I loved the comforts of no expectations. No added pressure.

Heat Wave! Summer in the Inland Empire would reach temperatures well over 100 degrees. That summer's heat laughingly showed us it could go higher. After realizing my dreams were pertaining to my friend, magically all of my dreams and weird occurrences stopped. My house felt peaceful again and cherry blossom and gardenia filled the atmosphere.

The summers came with a little flexibility in my schedule. Jihree spent a lot of time with his father; this helped lighten my day tremendously. Summer with its beautiful, long sunny days and long hot nights would always bring about the sensation of enjoying adult company.

Anthony was always there; we did not need a title. I appreciated our friendship and the ability to be myself. Our long, intimate and intellectual conversations always felt right.

At this point in our lives we had been friends for about six of seven years now, we discussed marriage lightly, but we were very comfortable with our lives.

He owned his own home. I owned my own. After spending time with each other, we gladly used our index fingers to point the way back to our own homes.

"You know I have to go to work. You have gas in your car? Do you know how to lock my door on your way out?"
We never took the comments personal. We enjoyed our honesty and friendship. I loved my space and he appreciated time with

his boys and his space.

On one cuddly hot day, Anthony and I enjoyed one of our open and playful conversations. His demeanor quickly changed as he sternly said, "Allissen!"

From the sternness of his voice I could tell the conversation was about to turn serious, something was really on his mind.

"What's up?" I replied.

I tried not to rush the conversation; however, I really wanted him to start babbling. I gently nudged him to speak by asking, "Is everything ok?" He began to expound,

"Do you remember the day we had your brother's anniversary party at my house?" he asked.

I replied, "Of Course I remember it was a couple of months ago." He continued in his explanation,

"Well, when you walked down the stairs I saw something!"

He was telling the story with entirely too much hesitation; I became alarmed. He continued:

"I don't want you to think this is weird, but when you came down the stairs you looked absolutely amazing, you had on all white and you looked gorgeous."

I rolled my eyes as I murmured,

"Well, thank you babe, but why was that hard to tell me?"

He took some small breaths and finished,

"But that wasn't all that I saw."

He took a breath in and blew out while changing his posture. I laid my head on his legs as we stared completely into one another's soul. I left a comfortable distance to allow him room to speak comfortably.

"Babe when you walked down the stairs, I saw something around you, behind you... it practically engulfed you." Reading my frustration, he rushed through his next statement,

"I saw an angel behind you, there was an amazing light behind you; you appeared to glow. There was an angel behind you, you were glowing."

Feeling at ease by his comments; however, I did not fully understand the meaning. I was eager to hear his interpretation of the vision; Anthony always had a way of knowing certain events before they would happen. The only understanding he could give me at that time,

"We will be married soon!"

His temperament was filled with determination, hope, love, peace and understanding. My perception in that moment was unimportant; I simply accepted in that moment, I did not need to fully understand the vision. The look in his eyes, which was a reflection of his soul sparkled. I understood he knew exactly what it meant and knew how to apply the meaning.

We sat as the noise in the silence permeated the room. He sealed his understanding with a kiss. We sat on the floor and appreciated each other's presence in the silence. My great night with Anthony continued with lots of laughs, great food and mind opening conversations. Our relationship felt so easy and right. We continued our beautiful night with sweet, soft kisses, which led to more sweet soft kisses. His hands remained soft after years of football and basketball. My smaller skin would gently rest on his softness, as I cuddled in his large frame.

His lips. His cheeks. His hands. His Mind. Yes, the nearness led to a very passionate night. I could melt into his large arms and body frame as I escaped the outside world. Our conversations, hearts and minds so open it enhanced our physical attraction. Breathing patterns in synchronized harmony. Our brown expressions tingled with vibrations as we made it our mission to cover every inch of our skin with gentle kisses.

The moonlight and our white smiles were the only light shining into the room. Our bodies glistened in the spears of the moons rays as our complexions entwined with the soft sheets.

"How can love like this be wrong?" In that moment, it did not matter as my self-talk broke through my indulgences briefly,

"God, do you want me to really knock someone out if I rush to be married again."

Quickly, able to hush up my guilt trip. I fully engaged my outward shell in the decadence as he satisfied my cravings.

I laughingly whispered,

"The angel speech got me, huh!"

The moon continued to climb to its highest peak and so did my friend and I.

While slowly catching our breaths as we floated down from our heights, Anthony blurted out,

"You're Pregnant!"

SCREEEEEEEEEEEEEECCCCCCCCCCCCCCCCCH! The sound of a record being scratched played in my head. Our intimate moment came to its conclusion in an unexpected twist. I instantly laughed because his timing could not be worse; I rolled my eyes and shared my thoughts,

"Geez, can I enjoy my moment a little while longer! Can I wake up first…better yet, go to sleep first."

He said, "No!" with no smiles.

Once again, the stern tone of his voice explained once again that his level of understanding was a little deeper than my own. He repeated, "You are pregnant and in a few weeks you will know." I continued to laugh as I tried to use my stern voice, "You Plotting on Me!!!"

The chuckling stopped as we cuddled in silence.

Being Mrs. Jones might be all right; however, I remained torn between doing the right thing and loving the peace and quiet of my home and my life.

I enjoyed the smells I created and changed at whim. I just simply enjoyed this time as a single woman. I attempted to convince myself that my choice was not a result of any residuals from my previous marriage. "God, I just enjoy my time for me and when the time was right, we would be ready."

The next morning did not feel any different, nor did it bring any different routines. I headed to work as usual and after work, I gladly returned to my own home. I continued in my usual and I did not think twice about the words Anthony uttered after our moment.

Halloween time forced me to spend some additional time at Wal-Mart near my job. After work, I pushed through the crowds and picked up some candy and a costume for my son.

While walking through the aisle I passed by the the feminine section and I realized I was missing something for that month. Quickly Anthony's words rushed in like a flood and I grabbed a pregnancy test. I ran into the bathroom after purchasing the test and the result of our passionate night laughed in my face. Positive.

"What, Positive!"

Gladly accepting the news; however, very perplexed at how Anthony knew instantly. I pondered on our previous conversation about seeing a light behind me and his ability to see us married soon. In that moment, my excitement about becoming a mommy again overshadowed my concerns.

Anthony and I discussed the news over dinner and of course it was of no surprise to him; although, he was highly upset about me calling him from a Wal-Mart bathroom with the results.

Over dinner, we did not discuss details about how our lives would change, nor how we were going to implement the changes. We still loved our comforts and our ability to somewhat control our world. We were reluctant to give up our illusion of control. I calmed any overwhelming feelings of being a single mother of two kids with my justifications:

> "Financially, I am secure. I owned my own home. My degrees were finished. My home and resources were large enough to support another kid. Anthony is genuinely a great person. He was financially secure, we have a great friendship and we value the same ideals on education and raising children...now there it is."

I accepted all of my justifications and we continued with my pregnancy without any hiccups. By November, we fully accepted, we would have a bouncing baby by July of 2008. Once again, Anthony blurted out,

"The baby will be born on June 18, 2008," I just shook my head.

The first trimester rolled by with morning sickness and slight fatigue. I was still in my routine working commercial real estate during the day and my own residential deals at night. My pregnancy required me to take additional naps, but other than that, all was well. My dreams stopped and my sleep during my pregnancy went uninterrupted. Fifteen pounds and six months later, my belly was nice and round. We gladly purchased blues and browns and picked out a date for our shower.

The spring of 2008, felt gloomy although a lot was in bloom. In some sense, I could feel everything was changing around me without asking for my input.

The real estate market was imploding; my deals took longer and required more time and more negotiation. I felt drained and the drainage had very little to do with my pregnancy.

Foreclosures were popping up at unbelievable rates. Lenders and banks that I built great relationships with, began to dry up and close their doors for good. Words like, 'the great depression' were coming out of the mouths of news reporters on a daily basis.

One heavy morning, I rolled out of bed to start my morning and headed to my nine-to-five. The drive there involved more traffic than usual; the drive took hours when it normally took forty-five minutes. I finally arrived and I was exhausted. The day was just beginning.

As I walked into the office, I could feel eyes staring at me and then turning away. Humm…it was obvious that something was going on, but what now.

I walked to my desk and some items felt out of place, a few

pictures moved and my computer pushed back. Before I could completely sit down, I heard my boss calling me into his office,

"Allissen the real estate market is imploding and I will have to let you go until I can figure some things out."

I knew from the heaviness I felt this morning, my tumultuous drive and the clouds in the sky something was brewing. I really did not have much to say, for the real estate market was a mess. I grabbed my banker box and packed my area.

As I was maneuvering around my belly to fill up boxes my feelings of dread caused tingling in my skin. My self-talk began,

"I cannot get another job while pregnant. I am about to have two boys with no consistent paychecks. What am I going to do about health insurance?"

My self-talk was interrupted by the eyes watching me box up my years spent with this company. I hurriedly boxed my items and left the building.

Driving home in the cloudy weather made the day feel strangely okay. I called Anthony and decided to meet him at his home. The instant change in control forced us to sit and discuss plans of our future seriously.

His home had decreased in value by almost 50% and it just no longer made sense for him to remain in a predatory loan.

We reluctantly decided to combine our homes. We would give it a few more months and then make the transition under one roof. My lay-off did not come with such a heavy blow, because I knew Anthony was 'all-in'. I could now enjoy the remainder of my pregnancy and operate my home business.

We sold his townhome and by the end of May, we settled into my home. We painted the baby's room and did all the required nesting; our lightness and ability to return to our own abodes were now a memory. The transition was not an easy one; however, we both silently knew the transition was necessary.

June 18, 2008!

Yes, Anthony predicted the correct date! Astonishingly he drove me to the hospital and once in front of the hospital my water broke. He pulled into the parking lot and my water broke in that second. Jelani Miles Jones was born five hours after Anthony pulled into the parking lot of the hospital for reasons he only understood.

There is nothing like a newborn baby in the house. I knew the importance of breast-feeding and there was no hesitation in my willingness to breast feed, even with the tremendous pain it caused me.

After one feeding, my left breast bled heavily, something was abnormally wrong. I regretfully prepared to stop breast-feeding. Shortly, after I stopped breast-feeding, I noticed a small lump on my left breast. I made an appointment with my gynecologist and he assured me;

"It is a clogged milk-duct; it will go away in time."

"You are young and healthy; it will go away in time."

Able to exhale after the appointment, I continued enjoying being a new mommy and adjusting to my new life with my partner. My pregnancy finally over, I was able to purchase another insurance policy designed for the self-employed. Anthony worked a regular scheduled job and I stayed home with the baby. We settled into our routine without any hiccups.

Christmas of 2008, Anthony proposed and I said 'YES!" The planning for a destination wedding in Jamaica began. We both always wanted to do things right in the eyes of God… this felt right and like a necessary step. I often reflected on our whirlwind situation over the last year and I really asked myself,

"Am I really ready to be married again?" My introspective moments were interrupted by wedding planning whoopla. Life must go on! Resorts to pick, dresses to decide on--no time for self-reflecting.

June 27, 2009!

Save the Dates sent and we had 6 months to make it happen. A large wedding was not our vision and with the wedding being in Jamaica, we knew we would get our wish of a small intimate wedding.

Jelani grew rapidly and time traveled along. I slept well at night; however, I still felt exhausted during the day. One day while Anthony was home with the baby. I finally soaked in a long hot bath. I extended my arm to reach for my shower gel and I felt some resistance. There was a tightness in my left arm. The pain and tightness caused great resistance; I had to grab under my arm with my hand. Once, I grabbed my underarm I touched two palpable lumps under my left arm. Instantly, my hot bath turned ice cold.

"What in the world?"

My heart raced and instantly I knew my clogged milk duct could not have moved under my arm, but I certainly hoped it could. My mother quickly encouraged me to make another appointment.

The coldness in the patient room was more perceptible than usual; my OB/GYN entered the room and everything from my point of view moved in fast-motion. The doctor felt my breast and then my underarm, pulled a stack of papers out and next had the audacity to say,

"You should have come in sooner."

The fast-motion halted. I struggled to control my anger and my tongue from lashing out at the doctor. My words came out in slow and deliberate motion:

"Dr. Yu, do you know how many times I came in here for you to look at my breast and you told me:

You are too young, you are African American and the prevalence is low, it is just a clogged milk duct. You are healthy, you are fine."

I was furious, scared as hell, and trying to anticipate the next move all at the same time. I knew from the tone in my doctor's voice and the stack of paperwork he completed and handed to me; this clogged milk duct was now very serious.

X-Ray. Ultrasound. Mammogram....Biopsy.

Biopsy day arrived and the biopsy room was cold. There was a large machine in the center with a screwdriver device on the end. I laid on the table and the technician numbed the area. The left side of my breast was partially numb and I could not help but stare at the device.

The machine turned on and made the sounds of a drill. The technician kept advising me to look away as this machine drilled into my left breast. The procedure took forever. I found a focus point to my right.

I spelled the name of the maker of the machine repeatedly. Once a small piece of my breast was removed, the technician gave me a smile,

"You know only a very small percentage of these come back positive."

I smiled and held on to the hope in her words and the kindness in her eyes. I gently placed my black tank top over the white gauze that now covered a hole in my left breast. I turned to my left to leave the room and a wheelchair was sitting by the door, as the technician insisted, "I must roll you out, Ms. Henry," Hesitantly, I shook my head to the left and to the right. My will stated, "No!" for this moment felt foreshadowing. I forcefully shook my head to the left and to the right, "No, I can walk." She would not hear me, "sorry, it is hospital policy." I sat in the chair just to get this moment over with. "Let's go!" The procedure room door opened and there I was in a wheelchair at thirty-one.

Yesterday, I was perfectly fine; you know what… two hours prior I was perfectly fine in my delusional shell.

"Why won't this clogged milk duct just evaporate and return my life. Give it back to me."

We rolled down a hallway where my parents and Anthony greeted me. Theirs smiles were filled with trembles as their mixed emotions impressed upon their faces.

Vulnerable. No covering. No Mask. Loss of identity all rolled in that black wheelchair. My eyes rolled from side to side in an attempt to pull from some parts of me. The independent me, I like her. The hard working me, she's bad. The unstoppable me, I needed her in that moment. Somehow, the me I was seeing was unfamiliar for I had never met a helpless me.

Fourteen days. Two-weeks. Three hundred and thirty-six hours. Twenty thousand-one hundred and sixty minutes and 1.2e+6 seconds. I laughed as I thought of what I would do with the space needed before my results were back.

I was supposed to sit and wait through each of these units used to measure choices, memories, life and death. Time felt like the worst four-letter word for it held power, beauty and dread.

"Alpha and Omega; the beginning and the end. All right, I know you have control of everything in the middle." I blurted as I tapped my fingers on my desk before I opened my bible.

Day One: I opened my bible and the page landed in Genesis and I read someone begot someone and then that someone begot someone else. It was all nerve-racking so I resorted to my cliché; "fix it Jesus!"

Day one ended with my closet color coordinated, wood floors polished, all the laundry completed and wood blinds dusted. My white gauze was now brown and red and I assumed I may have done a little too much as I passed out on my bed.

Day 7: My home was obsessively clean and Anthony would pull his clothing items from my hands to keep me from color coordinating his tank tops. I refused to work my way to the garage; therefore, by day eight I was forced to look Time in the face. I blew my lips until they made a vibration sound and rolled my eyes. Time just simply rolled on, as if to tell me, "You cannot avoid me." Fine, I will outsmart Time and the vulnerable me at the same time. "Wedding Planning! Ha-ha!" I will show Time the hopeful me as I picked out my Maggie Soltero wedding gown.

"Bam! In your face, life goes on."

My bright ideas kept coming,

> "Babe, we should have an engagement party and have the travel agent attend to answer questions."

Anthony agreed, therefore I began more planning. I created laminated invitations with information regarding our wedding location. 'Grand Palladium Resort & Spa in Lucea, Jamaica.' All right, life felt normal as we picked our wedding colors, discussed location and wedding planner.

> "Babe, what song do you want to dance too? What do you want to walk down the aisle too? How many people do you think will make it to Jamaica?"

I smiled for all of those questions did not really matter for I was marrying my best friend. Someone, whom I admired and loved in a passionate way. "Yes! Mostly the whole package." I closed my eyes as I stretched out against the bride magazines, passport applications for the kids and tons of other mind busying activities.

When my mind was not busying itself, flashes of my vivid dreams flickered before my eyes like an old movie reel. I had to fight feelings of regrets; thinking I may have missed something in a previous space of time.

"Maybe, the message was for me."
The vivid dreams and the unfamiliar presence in my home was trying to communicate something to me.
"Allissen you are tripping, the dreams felt like years ago."
I occasionally felt the lump protruding from my breast with the palm of my hand. I knew the clogged milk duct would heal. I could not allow myself to focus on regrets…I had a wedding to plan. Travel plans to make. Passports to get for
the baby and I needed to locate my own passport before the last hour.

The clogged milk duct would go away soon. Yep, it would go away soon.

February 19, 2009. The sun peaked through my blinds and planted a kiss on my eyes.

My morning call was on time, loud and clear. The cries from my son were not always nerve racking, for some odd reason I enjoyed his screams in the morning. The loud cries reverberated down the hall as the sounds bounced from the high ceilings and wood floors. "Jelani Miles Jones!" His screams would mellow to a weird groan once he heard my voice. Once I heard the weird sounds, which only a mother would love. I would peek my head into his room. His eyes looked through the rails of his crib in anticipation of me in his view. His eyes would grow bigger and his two teeth would shine through all the slobber. I jumped full body into his room and he burst into laughter. His laughter was contagious. I grabbed him as his legs waved back and forth in the joy of this place.

We laughed as I picked him up and planted kisses on his face and slobbery neck. I kissed, kissed and kissed his neck and my cell phone rang.

"Hello, this is Allissen...Oh' my test results were fine, great. Thank you! Thank you!"
I hung up the phone and continued to kiss my baby as we twirled in that span of time.

Bath-time! After news like that, mommy needed to soak. I ran the water and kept it lukewarm for us to enjoy together. I stopped the water a little above my waist to avoid wetting the hole in my left breast; the hole still oozed brown and red gunk. The lump was still present; however, the results were fine.

"Okay! Mommy is Okay," I whispered to Jelani.

We enjoyed beginning our morning in the tranquil sounds of water. His legs kicked, kicked and kicked to tell of the joy, he was unable to verbalize. The kicking continued as I laid him closer to my breast. I trickled water down his hair and watched it run across his cheeks. As I watched the water run pass his pure white eyes and blushing cheeks… my cell phone rang again:

"Hello Ms. Henry, the doctor wants you to come into the office immediately."

I responded hesitantly, for her previous actions and her new comments confused me.

"For what, I thought you said everything was fine."

The nurse stuttered,

"We-we just need you to come in."

We hopped out of the water, found some clothing and I loaded Jelani in his seat, I took some deep breaths and began the drive.

The wind against my face, helped distract my thoughts.

It was an amazingly beautiful day for February.

I parked, placed Jelani in his stroller and grabbed his diaper bag. The day felt normal; however, the sun was blazing on our faces, turning us both red.

He cooed softly in the sunshine as he cruised in his stroller. All of his necessities were in my hand as we entered the suite. Our expressions changed as we entered the building. The man -made architecture now veiled our sunshine. We reached our suite and the air near the door was cold and unwanted. We both sighed as we longed to go back into the sunshine.

Instantly, the room felt like a cold museum and I was on display. Large eyes, medium eyes, tight eyes, almond eyes and small eyes...eyes, eyes and more eyes all looked at me and through me.

My stomach sank. I could not hide, nor deny what I was feeling. I rushed to a seat to avoid passing out on the floor. Before I could sit my behind all the way down,

"Ms. Henry the doctor will see you now."

There was a short distance to the patient room and it felt as if eyes were watching my every move; in my peripheral, I could see my doctor moving very rapidly between the halls. I made it to the patient room, before I could sit down comfortably the doctor zooms in,

"It is not good news... you have breast cancer."

No context, no pretense, no foreplay, no warm- me- ups. No peppermint after for the horrible taste.

My mouth opened, jaws stiff as my salivary glands endeavored to help me swallow the lump in my throat. My hands extended as he piled paperwork on my arms like a stack of plates. The whirlwind of paperwork included cards, numbers to oncologist and surgeons. The world around me was moving in rapid motion. While, the world inside my head was absolutely stagnant.

My processing of information affected my every reaction…in… slow… motion.

Baby steps as I walked out of the exam room; every inch of me hurt. Physically hurt. Was I still in one piece? Fragments of me seen floating in the air, like a tossed 1,000-piece puzzle…I wanted my pieces back the way they were.

I could see the lips of the medical staff moving; nonetheless, the sounds were not registering. The noise of a tape recorder rewinding played in front of me and behind me. Mentally, I could not decipher the sounds.

The analytical side of me that is constantly analyzing my behavior is questioning,

"Am I actively attempting to disassociate?"
The news so unexpected and unreal that I refused to digest this information. In a blink of an eye, the world I knew had changed. I was standing at the counter with my son, his diaper bag on my shoulder; however, not knowing how I got here.

"How did I get here?"

The sound of nails scratching a chalkboard sent chills down my spine. My son's screams now pierced my ears and instantly, I was back in this dreadful moment. The nurse and doctor were babbling at this point, handing me appointment card after appointment card. Dr. Yu handed me one more card, smiled and wished me "good luck."

Their smiles irritated my core as rage cycled like a tornado fueled by every disappointment in my life. As the eye of the storm peaked near my heart, the hurt blew from my mouth like a dragon's fire directly at Dr. Yu:

"ARE YOU OUT OF YOUR MIND? I WISH YOU WOULD STAND THERE WITH A SMILE ON YOUR FACE! WHAT HAPPENED TO THE CLOGGED MILK DUCT? HUH! WHAT HAPPENED TO THE PREVELANCE BEING SO LOW IN AFRICAN AMERICAN WOMEN...UWWWW!
WHAT IF IT WAS YOUR DAUGHTER?
YOUR MOTHER?
YOUR SISTER?"

My view went dangerously red as images flashed before me with my hands around Dr.Yu's neck as I smashed his head against that clipboard he held, as he pretended to take notes.

"KEEP TRYING TO HIDE BEHIND THAT CLIPBOARD AND YOUR NOTES! YOU WILL SEE ME AND HEAR ME!"

I stood steaming in lava. I glanced down briefly at my son, and his two Bugs Bunny front teeth shined through the biggest smile. His two front teeth reminded me of his gigantic heart. I knew I could not snap Dr. Yu's neck today… not today.

Disconnected from the moment, I do not know how we made it out of the building. Same diaper bag. Same clothes. Everything around me appeared the same, but…but…but… nothing was the same. Outside the sunshine still had no effect. No change. The world around me was absolutely quiet.

My normal process of preparing to drive home felt the same; I strapped my son into his car seat and walked over to the driver's side. I placed my seat belt around my chest and grabbed the steering wheel. My hands trembled as if bolts of electricity shot down my spine as my adrenaline pulsated through my veins.

"I can't drive like this, calm down Allissen."

Sitting only made it worse for my thoughts were accumulating like snowflakes and the quietness caused one great avalanche:

"I told the doctors months ago and he said it was a clogged milk duct. No. No. No. this still has to be a clogged milk duct. I told the doctor months ago. I am only 31, how does this happen? What did I do to deserve this crap? How am I going to tell my son? I am supposed to get married in June! O'No! How am I going to tell Anthony! God, he saw his father die from cancer, now me! My... My life! I never bothered any one. I spent my life just doing what needed to be done. This is some bull-crap! Really, God, Really! Did I mention, I told Dr. Yu months ago!"
All of the traffic in my mind came to a huge collision as I yelled,

"God, I don't want to die! I don't want to die!"

Trembling from anxiety, confusion and anger, I sat in my car trying to pull it together to drive home. I would be happy to say the rumination stopped once my screams roared.

However, my cries only forced my son to join in as we both competed to have our waling heard by someone, anyone willing to listen. We cried in concert all the way home.

Arriving at home gave me little comfort only in knowing that we made it home. Driving while shaking, gushing out tears and profanity was a difficult task. My son's screaming stopped with a gentle touch and a dry ass. I watched him close his eyes for a nap; how I wished my problems were as simple as a dry ass.

I slowly walked to my room and slid down the side of my bed and like a lifeless lump of coal; I hit my cold floor. Somehow, the cold did not bother me. Did it matter? What really mattered?

I pulled my knees into my chest as my self-talk rolled in and created pressure in my ears. The water wells in my eyes began to empty as the tears ran across the center of my nose, where my glasses would normally sit. The drops from both eyes would entwine at my cheek, thus creating one big drop before pooling on the floor.

My moments or hours there still feel untraceable. I still cannot recall how long I was there frozen in fear. My trance interrupted by an abrupt new question and thought.

"Anthony will be home soon; what am I going to say? How am I going to tell him I have breast cancer?"

In a panic, I crawled off the floor and headed to my bathroom mirror. In the mirror, I squinted my eyes for my reflection was obscured by mascara running down my face; the tears formed shadows around my eyes. The right side of my hair was soaked from my puddle of sorrow. Hastily, I washed my face and slammed my make-up kit on the counter in an attempt to mask my pain and confusion. I grabbed my M.A.C. foundation in a struggle to hold together the broken pieces and my shame.

I pulled my hair back. Applied new mascara. New foundation. New blush and New lip-gloss. I practiced my words and my tone as I prepared my expressions to leave an

outward impression of strength. "Hold it together, Allissen!"
Back and forth. Back and forth. Back and forth. Back and forth.
I paced up and down the side of our bed and rehearsed the lines
and the way to tell him, over and over. As I paced the floor, a
feeling of dread came over me as my self-talk continued:

> "It took forever for him to discuss the death of his father
> from cancer and he still lives in the trauma of that
> experience at times. He will not step a foot into a
> hospital…I can't do this to him, I-I can't!"

I continued to pace for the time was drawing near for him
to arrive home. I walked from the side of our bed, headed to the
bathroom mirror in an attempt to present to him the person he
once knew. My pacing continued and suddenly, I could hear the
loud rolls of the garage door as it slowly began to lift.

> "Oh! What am I going to do? Maybe I should not tell
> him! We can go on with life as we were…
> let's keep planning the wedding and our lives will go
> on!"

Denial never worked for me and I knew nothing was the same.
My life was forever changed and no one asked me if I was
ready, nor for my permission--
No one asked me if I was ready.

Abruptly, I could hear the garage door rolling down and the
house door slam. My pacing and practicing of my outward

strength became more rapid. My heart raced. I turned to leave my bathroom mirror to continue my pacing, I looked to my right and there he stood...There he stood.

A flood of heat rushed from my head to my toes.

"God, it has to be impossible to feel this many emotions at one time."

Love. Friendship. Panic. Hope. Misperception. Victimization. False sense of strength. Sorrowfulness and Fear crept from my core to the outward most layer of my skin causing redness. I tried and I tried to push the emotions out by shaking my hands vigorously in the air.

Once he entered the room my quotes and outward strength I attempted to muster slowly dissipated. In my mind, I still held on to the quotes; but, out of the valves in my heart exploded:

"Just leave me! Please, I do not want you to endure any pain! Just leave me! I love you too much to cause you anymore pain!"

The pieces were too broken for the foundation to hold together. I just couldn't hold it together any longer. The pain leaked through my waterproof mascara as I struggled to hold on to something that was in my control...even if my strength was an illusion.

The tears and foundation poured as I continued to hold on to something...even if it was just my baggage.

"Just leave me! I will be okay! I will beat this! You know I will beat this! Sometimes things just don't work out. We will forever be friends. But I will be ok!"

The ball of emotions swirled in the center of my being like a tornado, actually causing me physical pain. The mental anguish hurt. The agony forced me to my knees. I crumbled. In the middle of crumbling, our faces met in the same space of time. Anthony's eyebrows slightly raised as if he too were pulling from something inside. His stature tall, but shaky. His lips trembled as he held back his own tears; his fist were balled tight as he stood in a fight posture.

As we shared this space, the sweet and familiar face of my friend was present. His face mirrored an expression I came to enjoy. One of acceptance, love, peace and endurance. In that moment, somehow I knew... I knew, he knew long before he looked upon the brokenness on my face.

Anthony cleared his throat. I waited for his words as I rummaged through my baggage and prepared to handle this trial on my own. He walked in closer to my face, knelt down in his gentle manner and spoke:

"I'm about to go to the store for some Kleenex and make-up remover for all those colors on your face, but I am coming right back home."

That night we ate Spaghetti and salad.

My first appointment with an Oncologist scheduled. I set-out to understand more about breast cancer through my internet research before my appointment.

"Wow, it looks as if there are three… maybe four different types of breast cancer. I did not know that. Geez, I hope I have the one with the higher survival rates."

I could not believe I was making that statement at thirty-one.

The Internet is a scary place at times. I read information from reputable sources. I studied the different types and the treatment protocols for each. I learned new words to me like neo-adjuvant versus adjuvant; differentiated, undifferentiated. ER+, PR+, Her2neu+, and Triple Negative. The statistical information was overwhelming. I decided to educate myself about the disease only and read about death rates later, or maybe never.

Appointment day, I now hoped for an early stage and an easily treatable form of breast cancer.

"Hi, I am Dr. Lewis, Medical Oncology."

After the formalities, we begin to discuss breast cancer openly.

"Allissen, at this time your tumor is 3.7 cm and we need to treat your entire body."

"Okay, Dr. Lewis so I need neo-adjuvant treatment?
I asked.

"Yes, Allissen we need to treat your entire body at this stage."

He opened my pathology report and his facial expression changed. He touched my shoulder and began to explain to me:

"Allissen, you have a very aggressive form of breast cancer (Her2neu+) and the morbidity is very high. The sample we removed from your breasts showed very little, if any normal cells, this means that the area is undifferentiated."

I quickly interrupted him and asked,

"Dr. Lewis, undifferentiated…very little or no original breast cells were present in my sample. It was all malignant?"

"Yes, Allissen, this cancer is moving fast."

My heart skipped beats, for I hoped for a simple surgery and no chemo. I forced myself to stay in the room with Dr. Lewis as my mind wondered to Disneyland, a beach or some other place…any place, but here.

My self-talk shouted in my mind…"Focus, Allissen," as I attempted to drift right on out of that place in time. I tried to absorb the information as he spoke, but my goodness I was experiencing sensory overload.

Dr. Lewis continued:

"Allissen, we are delayed in detection, so we are up against the clock. I need you to begin chemotherapy as soon as possible. Surgery at this point may help, but at your stage we need to treat the entire body."

I quickly responded," Let's start, Dr. Lewis!"

The doctor's eyes looked down on the floor and then up to me and he stated,

"I need you to call your insurance company."

"Okay" this must be part of the process. I agreed and continued to schedule my appointments for our next visit.

"I will see you in a few days, Dr. Lewis"

Doors slammed loudly in the car.

That was the only sound made during the 1:20 minute ride home with Anthony. No radio. No Questions. The magnitude of our trial was beginning to take shape; albeit, it still felt surreal.

In the silence, mentally I began to prepare a to-do-list and of course at the top of my to-do-list,

"Call the insurance company."

I made it home and ran into my office with a sense of eagerness; I was ready to begin treatment. I sat at my glass desk in my office and made the call.

A young pleasant and bubbly Customer Service Representative answered, *"Hi Ma'am"* I quickly began to jabber and once the hellos were over, the remainder of the conversation was one I never expected:

"Ma'am, your oncologist put in a request for chemotherapy treatment, and Ma'am, when you completed your paperwork there was a small check-box at the bottom of the paper. You did not check that small box. So, therefore chemotherapy is not included in your coverage."

"Huh? What did you say? Can you repeat that?"

"Ma'am, I said, chemotherapy is not covered."

The blood began to rush to my head, my ears, and my fingers. I could feel heat rising from the center of the earth. For my world was about to implode. I tried not to pop. I took a deep breath and with all sincerity, I asked,

"Well fax it to me. I will check the missing checkbox. I will fax it back to you. Just a missing checkmark, we can figure out an easy solution."

"Ma'am I will not be able to do this, because you now have a diagnosis. You now have cancer. Your cancer diagnosis is now classified as a PRE-EXISTING CONDITION. There is nothing we can do."

"Lady, Ma'am…what's your name again? You reiterated the fact that I have cancer. Let us say that again…Cancer! So you do you understand I have Breast CANCER, Not a HEADACHE! I have been paying premiums to you, and now I need services? I do not recall the Salesmen explaining this little checkmark that I missed, nor did he point out this box when I purchased the policy. I need you to fax it to me today. I will fax the MISSING CHECKMARK to you today so I can begin chemotherapy soon."

"Ma'am, I cannot fax anything to you because, you… will… not be COVERED!"

The Santa Ana winds blew from my nose as I struggled to blow out my frustrations. Feelings of anger and dread caused me to stand up out of my office chair and hunch over the telephone. My whirlwind of emotions begin to spin around-around-and around.

My emotions ranged from wanting to fight like a caged animal to pleading for my life. I held on to the edge of my desk as if someone were about to throw me off a cliff. I bit hard on my shirt to stop the expletives from projecting like vomit.

"LADY, I just gave birth to my son and I have another son and he is twelve. The doctor is telling me I have a very aggressive form of cancer. I do not have any time to waste. We need to get moving. Tell me what you need from me."

"Ma'am, I have told you there is nothing we can do for you at this time."

The room became tight and with every word this woman spoke, my posture cowered lower and lower. I was kneeling on one knee as I attempted once again to have this lady connect to me and what I was facing:

"Lady, I can send you pictures of my kids, I am sure you already have reports from my oncologist. THIS IS GOING TO KILL ME! I need to begin treatment. I am already late stage. I CAN'T! I CAN'T DIE! Who is going to take care of my kids? Let me repeat myself very slowly.

I-Have-Breast-Cancer and I- Need –My –Health – Insurance –to –do –what they- are- supposed to do."

I was on my knees pleading for my life as if someone where standing over me with a loaded gun. My desperate pleas for help created NO CHANGE, NO EMOTION and NO HELP. The representative's tone remained the same and dry as hell:

"Is there anything else I can do for you, Ma'am? Is there anything we can do for you ma'am?"

Why! Why! Why! Why! Why! Why! Why!

Did she open her mouth one more time! Why? Before I could stop the muscle called my tongue, there was an instant spasm:

"**IF YOU CALL ME MA'AM ONE MORE TIME!
JUST ONE MORE TIME!
HELP ME! HELP ME!
GIVE ME ALL MY GOT-DAMN PREMIUMS BACK!
ALL OF THEM!
TAKE MY MONEY AND NOT OFFER HELP WHEN
NEEDED!
THE SALES REP DID NOT POINT OUT SOME SMALL
ASS CHECK MARK!
THIS IS SOME CRAP I NEVER EXPECTED.
THE SYSTEM IS SCREWED!
MONEY, MONEY, AND MONEY!
WHAT ABOUT LIVES? WHAT ABOUT MY LIFE?
DO MY KIDS NOT MATTER!
EEEEEEEEEEEEEWWWWWWWWWWWWWWWW
WWWW!
IF I EVER CATCH YOU ON THE STREET;
I AM GOING TO WHOOP YO' ASS!**"

By the time I could catch my breath, all I heard was the dial tone.

"The dial tone, really. Really, REALLY!"

This just infuriated me more; phone in hand, I got off my knees to dial the number again to finish my rant. My tears streamed with anger as I frantically dialed the number again.

I looked out at the corner of my office and Anthony and Jihree stood in the doorway. "AWW, hell!"

Naked Allissen, vulnerable Allissen and ashamed Allissen looked passed the bewilderment on their faces. I mentally shouted,

"I cannot be 'figure–everything-out' Allissen right now!" I could not answer their questions, nor stare too long. I had to get back to cussing someone out. Someone was going too finally listen to me.

"Who would I really ask for and who would I look for to beat down?"

Frantically, I dialed the number and slid my office chair across the room to close my office door. I did not want my son to learn any new words. I reached out my hand to slam the door and Anthony grabbed my hand with force. Already beyond fury, I snarled at him,

"Let my hand Go!"

He would not. He pulled me in close.

I yanked my arm back and pushed him away for the necessity of calling the insurance company was of prime importance. Nothing else mattered.

Anthony grabbed my phone;

"She is not the battle, focus on the real battle."

I growled at him;

"Said the man who does not have cancer!

No- No- No! I have to call her back. This is my only hope! I don't want to DIE! I don't want to die! I have to get back to Customer Service Rep..... #1245! Whatever her name is."

My hysterical state flared up panic in my child as Jihree screamed, "What is wrong, Mommy? Mommy, what is wrong?"

From surreal to real in seconds.

Blowing up the insurance company would not help me at this point. My child's voice had a way of snapping me back to reality. The weight on my shoulders forced my body to hit the floor with a loud thud. I sat in a stupor.

My last thought of hope was looking around waiting for the camera crews to enter. "Come on camera crew!"

I must be on an episode of Punked!

I waited on Ashton Kutcher to enter my room or Big Boy to say it was a phone tap!

No one, NO ONE! NO ONE!

Just my nakedness and me.

My knees caved into my chest in an attempt to support this unbelievable strain on my shoulder. This whole process was becoming too much:

"I give! Time-Out! I am ready to wake up now! Time -Out! Can I get a break? Just one! Just one God!

This was real fun and funny, now it is time to wake up."

As much as I wished I were in a dream state this was my reality and what my world had come too in a matter of days. Days! I crawled to a corner near the bluest wall in my office. I buried myself in the tightness of the diagonal space, in an attempt to conceal the shadow of someone I once was and a life I once knew.

I squeezed close in the corner, legs and arms wrapped tight as I attempted to disappear.

Disappear.

The Valley

Tick-Tock; Tick-Tock, Tick-Tock. Tick---Tock, Tick---Tock, Tick---Tock, Tick-Tock. Tick-Tock, Tick-Tock, Tick. Ti-ck-to-ck.

The seconds on the clock where piercing, intimidating and paralyzing. Benumbed by the weight of my plight; I sought concealment within my own belly. My body cowered into a fetal position with my head hidden within my defeat.

I sat in the very narrow corner of my office staring into the darkness. In the darkness the rumination welcomed me. I could not stop the flood of thoughts that now filled my mind from slowly seeping from my head. The energy in my thoughts swirled around the room like mist.

The life in the air was dissipating, completely altering the atmosphere of the room.

I could not breathe.

I was suffocating. Slowly the room became small and smaller. Tight and tighter.

The square shaped room now felt like a rubric's cube with me in the middle surrounded by unorganized colors and patterns with no solution. Every manipulated turn caused more disorganization in my square. I could not stop the tears, nor the confusion as I sat in the chaos.

I tussled in the darkness with my mind leading the way. I sensed a door open, someone was attempting to enter.

I remained naked attempting to understand cause and effect;

"How did I get here? What did I ever do?"

The gavel pounded in my mind three times as the judicial process was called to order.

I placed myself on trial.

Once I opened myself up to indictment, the Prosecutor entered in the darkness. His hollow voice heard like piercing screams. His walk was slow and calculating as his footsteps echoed the sounds of chains. The Prosecutor was cunning and relentless with accusations:

"Where is your attorney?

Are you defending yourself?

Where is your God?

Were those stripes for you?

You deserve this, because you are a failure!

Somehow, you did something wrong, go ahead and admit it! Are you living with Anthony?

You are going to die!

Start picking mothers for your kids!

Where is your Jesus? No help is coming. Just give in!

Make it quick!

Come on. Come on. Think back to all the things you have done. Healer, where is he? Not coming for you! "

The accusations would not cease and were offensively clamorous.

The Prosecutor hammered in one after the other. Bombarded with past choices, past failures, and past hurts. I stammered out my justifications; however, my defense was weak for it lacked understanding of truth. The Prosecutor attempted to devour me once he knew he had my attention, my mind turned to him.

I cowered in my position, as my past choices were drilled into me one by one.

Near the place of exhaustion, the accusations resembled truth.

"Just stop! Just go away!"

I had no strength to yell overruled, badgering the witness, or that is enough!

The precocious sounds of the gavel of judgement continued hitting the chambers of my heart relentlessly.

I began to create my own sentence:

"I will end my engagement to Anthony today.

My baby does not know me all that well just yet, he can come to know another mother figure.

I will just lock myself in my room until it is over.

My firstborn has developed a great relationship with his father over the last couple of years.

Okay, Okay this is the way I am going to die."

Once, the Prosecutor felt his prey was weak, he went in for the kill. His boasting and grand standing increased to an outrageous high. The Prosecutor continued in an unnecessary wrath, for I was already broken and near the place of writing out my own guilty plea.

The accuser spoke one more accusation, which shook the chambers of my heart as he flashed pictures of my eldest son. Tauntingly he danced with the picture and in his maniacal voice,

"Since you failed; He Is Mine!"

His teeth shaped like nails. His breath full of rotting lies.

"Since you failed; He is Mine!"

"Since you failed: He is Mine!"

"Since you failed; He is Mine!"

My body trembled. I knew my Accuser had an ostensible advantage. The trembling this time did not begin on the outside, this roaring was from my core. My inner man trembled; but not from trepidation. This tremble filled with the vibrations of love was rising from my inner man. The power of love looked through the picture of my child and gawked into the darkness of my accuser's eyes. Our eyes locked.

The emptiness of his hollow voice and the foul smell of his judgements no longer caused me to cower; he was not my arbitrator.

In this plane of decisions flashes of Hezekiah being sick unto death moved quickly before me. I could see Hezekiah turn his face to the wall. The wall. The wall.

The wall, an obstacle that may look unmovable. Hezekiah turned his face to the wall and prayed. He faced the obstacle and prayed to the Lord. I drew strength from truth.

The accuser still jeered a picture of my son in my face. My eyes now twinkled with sarcasm,

"Keep on talking to me like I, I mean We, that we means you and me don't have a God. For every knee shall bow."

He continued in his hollow accusations as if I was unaware of all the walls that have been made to waste, by calling on the name of the Lord.

My eyes now connected to the love in my son's eyes. I could no longer stomach the foul odor of condemnation. Through my son's eyes a love grew inside of me. I looked at this wall attempting to separate me from my life force.

"How do I get to my life force? I know in him I live and breathe. But where are you?"

I looked through the wall I was allowing the father of lies to erect, with all my being, inner and outer man connected, I wept forcefully;

"LORD, CHRIST JESUS, HEAR MY CRIES!"

Forcefully, with the strength of a thousand mothers pulling my arms and the determination of a bull. I burst through the cubed walls stoned in despair, confusion and condemnation. From the bluest corner of my office, I crawled and slid out from the shadows to my nearest light. With the turn of my hand, the darkness was temporarily gone. Exhausted. Eyes red and swollen. I had to find some help.

"Jesus, help me lead me in the right direction."

My Internet search began with calling the American Cancer Society and they were able to give me a local resource. I called the Desert Cancer Project and they had certain income limitations and they generally assist with one or two treatments.

Next, I called the Cancer Centers of America. I had no problem beginning my conversation with,

"Help Me! I have no insurance and no major money!" The representative quickly informed me of the dollar amounts needed to begin and the number was so astronomically high my first response was,

"Do you have payment plans?" the representative chuckled and stated,

"That would be the first installment."
Bordering between the blurred lines of sanity, I laughed as well. Ok, on to the next avenue.

Phone call, after phone, after phone call, after phone call—no glimmer of hope. First question always asked of me was for insurance information and then the cost was explained. I had to fight the tightness and the foul odor from returning in the room. I continued to type and type. Research and research.

Hours passed and no help reached me.
The sun went down and every inch of my office floor was

covered in phone books, print outs and my notes. I held pieces of asphalt, but not one complete road to a solution.

The sun slowly retreated for the day and there I sat with my papers, phone books and internet pages. I refused to return to my nearest blue corner; albeit, the shadow followed me. I pulled my knees into my chest as I listened to the flutters of Time.

Tick-Tock, Tick- Tock, Tick-Tock.

Time was flying and would not ease up to give me more time to think my way through.... I just needed to think my way through.

Doctor's appointments scheduled; however, no movement. No treatment. No surgery. I attempted to remain hopeful and I continued my search for help.

My next appointment with my oncologist, he explained the cost of chemotherapy and the type of services I would need in addition to chemotherapy.

He also explained, surgery should be done after chemotherapy due to the late stage of my diagnosis. We were looking at several tens of thousands per month, I would need chemotherapy every three weeks.

He explained chemotherapy could run between $30,000 and $40,000 with each session, after chemotherapy the injection I needed was $7,000.00. Depending on the tumors response and if I remained healthy enough for treatment, I would be looking at six to twelve treatments. After, the initial chemotherapy sessions, I needed a bio-targeted chemotherapy for a full year. I would also be looking at 36 sessions of radiation.

The amount of money required was astronomical. Looking at the cost, I wanted to understand my chances as I asked, "Would it work? Dr. Lewis, Would treatment work?"

"Allissen, at your stage and the aggressiveness of your cancer, chemotherapy may extend your life, by months or possibly a couple of years. However, we will not know until after the first couple of treatments."

I shook my head as I wrapped my mind around his words "Great chemo will just be giving me a little more time for a whole bunch of money."

We discussed surgery as an option and we learned my lymph nodes were involved so removing the breast was not enough to treat the cancer. Dr. Lewis completed his wonderful news and offered more glorious news,

"Eighty-five percent of women with your diagnosis are dead within two years and, and you are already late stage. Also, this cancer loves the brain."

The words from my doctor were blatant…

Leaving the appointment we ran; we did not walk straight to the Department of Social Services.

"Ma'am, I need to apply for medi-cal."

Pride on the floor. I looked for any help available to me.

The application was long and a lot of financial information was needed. I owned my own home and since the age of twenty-seven, I was making well over six figures, therefore:

DENIED!

All of our outside resources were exhausted at this point. Anthony and I, left the appointment with our heads down and unable to look at each other without crying. We were able to catch eyes from time to time only for a moment. To look into his eyes too long made the situation too real. Making it home and walking inside felt unfamiliar.

The world I knew vanished. Vanished right before my eyes.

"How can this happen in America? I completed school, I pay taxes, and I did everything I was supposed to do! Now, I need help! Where do I go for help?"

I sat and thought of ways to manipulate the system... I can put my house in my mom's name. I sat and figured out ways to show, I'm completely broke and then maybe I would get some help. But the reality of it was, I was racing against Time... Time was winning.

I went home and I knew I had exhausted every option known available to us at this point. I could not find another resource in this world.

I literally turned to the right and hit a brick wall. I turned to the left and hit a rubber barrier, the rubber barrier bounced me into a bed of thorns. As, I tried to get out of the thorns my feet stepped into quicksand. To avoid sinking I had to hold on to the thorns and watch my hands bleed.

There I was sinking and bleeding. Trapped in my reality. No escape. No retreat.

"Life, Life, Life!"

My kids still needed me. Baby needed to be changed. Homework and football practice. Dinner and laundry. Hugs and kisses. Breakfast and lunch. PTA and teething.

Existing between my reality and what I tried to present to my children gave me moments of living. Simple moments of making eggs and bacon or preparing to feed my infant would resemble a life I knew just days ago.

Conflictingly, the same moments that resembled living were filled with tears, frustration, and resentment. No matter how much I tried in those moments, I was unsuccessful at making Time stands still.

It just would not stand still. "Just be still."

Time was moving.

Slowly, accepting that my end was near, my bright ideas popped in my mind like popcorn. Feeling adept in managing my world; the first light bulb went off and I accepted,

"I will slowly disappear from my children's lives. I will take to the seclusion of my room as much as possible."

In my irrational-rational mind, I felt this would make their lives easier when I died. My plan was to remain difficult and contrite and become peevish, forcing them to avoid me as well. My aloofness would ease the pain when I passed. Sounded like a great plan at the time; however, my firstborn always found his way into my room.

"Why is everything such an arduous task, can I not hide with ease? Don't you know I am hiding from you?" Reminders of time were everywhere, just like the wind. Diapers and adamant love from kids made that plan very practical. "What's next? Little Brainiac."

Sleep, what was that? Sleep, interrupted by constantly looking over at Anthony or walking down my hallway to look in on my boys. First peeking in on my baby and then my eldest. Their sleeping faces gave me temporary comfort for they looked so peaceful, safe, secure, and rested.

The solace was quickly removed and my qualms replaced the comfort as I grumbled,

"How can they lay there asleep? Don't they know what I— what we are facing?"

As I walked away from their rooms, I ventured down my stairs; I passed the lively pictures on the walls. The frames held the happiness, hopes and life that once permeated the atmosphere.

Slowly passed those days, I retreated to my narrow blue corner in the darkness of my office.

No slumber. No food. Just day-dreams of a life I once knew in an attempt to avoid this present life.

The time was 1:33 a.m. and the atmosphere in my home was cave-like quiet. When, I finally made a sound, it would echo throughout the walls. The eerily quiet atmosphere in my home was completely opposite to the internal workings in my head. For in my mind, played the thunderous sounds of an orchestra.

The rear section was composed of loud horns raging sounds of resentment. The right section filled with cellos and bases, bellowed the same tune of anger over, over and over. To the left, the percussions, harp and first violin added their thuds and screeching crashes of disbelief. The disharmony of all the loud notes and chords on repeat forced me outwardly to place my hands over my ears. My hands tightly cupped my ears in an unsuccessful attempt to stop the inward noise. My eyes moved to the left side to hear the roars of disbelief and then to the right in my anger.

There I took a pew in this uncanny outward quietness, while internally suffering from calamity and disharmony.

Second after second. Minute after minute. Hours and Hours. Day in and Day out.

Brooding on a life I once knew, flashes of my previous dreams became very vivid. Recapitulating my dreams caused me to regretfully shake my head, "the dreams were pertaining to me and I missed it." Knowing, I could not take any more punches, I avoided beating myself up more for not paying attention. I played the dreams, methodically in an attempt to discern the important intersections.

In an A-HA moment somehow, the time stuck out to me, "3:00 a.m., but why was that important? Why was that important?"

My dreams ended between 3:00 am and 3:15 a.m.

I did not fully know the significance of the time; however, I decided to begin prayer at that time for as many days as I had remaining.

"I know there was something spiritual regarding 3:00 am and whatever was communicating to me, chose that time to speak...3:00 a.m. it is!"

I did not want to gather my understanding of the time from worldly understandings or the meaning I gathered from horror movies. I simply decided to begin my prayer-time at 3:00 a.m. for whatever was being communicated during my dreams always spoke during that time.

At this point my awareness of my relationship with God would not allow me to welter in despair. I momentarily would make pit stops in Despair Alley. Why Me Road? Resentment

Cove and Doom and Gloom Lane. Laughingly, with my wry sense of humor, I would walk down ALL these roads during my prayer sessions.

I opened my bible and nothing jumped out. I researched all the healing scriptures and they gave me short comfort. I pleaded with God:

"Please, God, I cannot sleep. I cannot eat.
There is something in my body and I can't track it. I can't see this tormentor, called cancer. I don't know where it is, nor how much longer it has before taking my life.
Lord, I know we wrestle not against flesh and blood.
It is now my own body that has turned against me. The enemy is within."

My first 3:00 a.m. prayer time was unsuccessful and really felt like a continuation of my pity party. I concluded prayer-time or whatever you would call that, and headed back up into the seclusion of my room.

I closed the door to the outside world.

I continued to find ways on my own to make my transition smoother. I held on to my illusion of control by deciding on who I would like to see as mother-figures to my boys.

I chuckled as I thought of all the women Anthony would have to fight off. I just decided to help him out by making a list of the ones that would make me peek down from heaven to show my face if he ever-ever-ever had them in the presence of my children.

I knew in some way everyone would eventually be fine.

I took great joy in knowing that my ex-husband and our firstborn were now very close. I even smiled at knowing my ex-husband had a stable girlfriend and she loved my son. My son now had brothers to walk through life with.

"Maybe the last several years were all to prepare for my death. Are you ready for me to walk upon the clouds? Are you calling me home, Lawrd?"

It all sound great; however, my comments were riddled with clichés…For I knew you called me to walk upon the waters in this world, but where is all the power you said we would have? "Where is it Lord?"

I continued with ways of my own. I decided to prepare letters for my children to read every morning. I took out several large boxes of pictures. In my seclusion, I began to write letters to my kids. I sought to have words for them every single morning they opened their eyes.

"I am yours and you are mine, forever."

I struggled to write a date at the beginning. Writing a date on the letters was morbid; in the recesses of my mind, I was subtly accepting the inevitable.

"Would I still be here in six months? A year…two?"

My self-talk only caused a brief delay in completing my task for the words of my doctor clang in my ears,

"This cancer loves the brain-This cancer loves the brain" played constantly in my head. His words fueled my writing,

"Let me write all that I need to say now, while my brain still functioned. I will outsmart Time."

I wrote to my boys and I even added a little elusive bargaining with God as I dated my letters for two-years down the road.

Dear Jihree,

I hoped to write a letter for you to read, every morning you opened your eyes.

However, that was a huge task. LOL!

I did not know what date to place on this letter, so go ahead and add that date as you read.

I hope you are doing better than expected and you have lots of friends. You know, I take that back...I hope you have a few really good friends. Good friends are hard to come by.

I will jot down my feelings daily or weekly.

I love you and I am always near.

Jelani Miles Jones,
(Mighty one)
My baby with the most energy,
you kept me going. I don't know
where I found the energy some
days to keep up with you.
Are you still sucking your fingers?
You know you entered this world
with those fingers in your mouth!
I hope your brother or dad is
reading this to you.
In a few years you will be able to
read it on your own.
I know your grandmother will
have you reading by two.
I love you with and unchanging
love.
Mommy

I only made it through one set of letters;
"God if I can just have five more years, please just five more years."

After my pleas, I remained very still with my letters in hand. In complete silence, I wished.
Out of the silence I heard a voice,
"And in five years what would you do then?"

I looked around my place of seclusion.
"Huh, where did that voice come from?"

I continued to remain silent with hopes that it would speak again. I closed my eyes. I waited a few minutes and opened one eye in anticipation. However, to my dismay… just silence. Tick-tock. Tick-tock. Tick-tock.

The hours flew. The world outside my seclusion continued as if nothing changed. "How was practice, Jihree," asked Anthony. I could hear the laughter from Jihree as he discussed his day with Anthony. My precocious little one kept the house in an uproar. The hustle and bustle of settling him down after a long day, could be draining and memorable simultaneously. I could clearly hear life happening all around me.
I remained in hiding.

My capricious disposition caused me to laugh within seconds of crying.

Ironically filled with much despair. I set my alarm clock to 3:00 a.m. for prayer. One morning as I headed to my office for prayer, I clearly heard that voice again. The voice was stern but laughingly whispered,

"You might as well stay in your bed.
What good does it do to pour new wine in old wine skins?"

Cantankerously, I responded; (I really did not even listen to the question being asked)

"Because I want to know why! Why Me? I never smoked!
I am not a bad person, why me? Half the
times, I don't bother anyone, I keep to myself!"

I blurted out my response as loud as I could and waited on a response. Nothing, absolutely nothing!
Just silence!

"OK- OK, Lord going to ask me a question and then be quiet, Thanks a lot! Answering our questions should be an obligatory function of my God, right??"

I remained in my office determined to finish out my 3:00 a.m. prayer time; I needed some clarity, a scripture, a sign, a rainbow or something.
"Where am I missing it?"

My stubbornness was flagrant as postured like a bull. I decided to sit there as long as it took for God to answer.

"Talk to me!"

As I sat in the dimness of the room with my stubbornness chiseling the definition of my face. My resentment was unfolding creating a hunch on my back.

No answers were spoken…so I returned back to listening to my own answers.

I thought of all the choices I may have made in life and how they somehow warranted this outcome.

"If I could just get understanding of this thing, then in some way it may help with my acceptance."

I continued to draw from my worldly understanding to solve my dilemma.

"Smoking, I never smoked. I had my occasional shots of tequila and of course my male adult time…but my Lord, Really!"

My self-talk continued as I babbled on and on:

"Okay Lord, Okay, this the consequence of some action of my own. Curse without cause will not come. I have heard that all of my life. But what did I do to deserve this?"

I could feel my countenance descend and the room darkened and felt constricting. In the darkness, I heard the clashing of teeth.

The Accuser was trying to build his argument again as he waited for me to acknowledge his presence. I shook my index finger while speaking,

"You roam seeking whom you may devour. 'May' denotes you need entry or permission. Today you are not invited in…away with you. Not today!"

This bombardment of thoughts about my past was not of God and it was a tactic to keep me from the original question presented to me earlier.

"What good does it do to pour new wine into old wine skin?"

I was frustrated with the parables, the quotes, and the clichés. So much talk, but I needed an answer to fall on my lap. "Blah….Blah…Blah…Blah!"

"I GET IT GOD, IF YOU POUR NEW WINE IN OLD WINE SKIN, IT WILL NOT BE PRESERVED…YEAH, YEAH, YEAH! HOW DOES THAT HELP ME NOW! NOW!"

I left my office and prayer time with absolutely nothing as I mumbled,

"You were absolutely right and I should've stayed in my bed. I concur!"

Once I returned to my place of seclusion and the torture chamber, I now called my bed.

I crawled under my unfamiliar sheets and in some way wished I could crawl under the mattress. Better yet, just go under my bed.

I was unable to stop the lively and colorful parade of my past from marching through my thoughts. When the parade did stop it was only to focus on the tumor protruding from my chest. I decided to stay under the covers for the remainder of the day. Who was I hiding from at that point, I don't know. Maybe, just maybe I was attempting to hide from myself.

I could not eat. I could not sleep. I often wondered if positioning on my left side would cause the tumor to travel faster to other organs.

"Where is this cancer? My breast? My head hurts, my back hurts? Is the cancer there?"

12:00 a.m., 2:00 a.m., 2:30 a.m., 2:45 a.m., 2:52 a.m. Time did not matter because the torture was ruthless. My face clammy. Eyelids wide open. Hair washed in sweat. The tear shaped sweat rolled down my forehead in rhythm. I remained frozen in my perspiration. Trying not to move.

"Don't move Allissen, just be still!"

I laid frozen in my exudate as I had to face my tormentor. I did not know where the cancer was, nor where it was traveling. My eyes rheumy as I stared into the darkness looking for this tormentor.

"I know he is lurking around, but where?"

I strained my eyes in an attempt to see. I used my free right hand to feel blindly around my body, starting with the lump on my chest. Next I move down towards my nipple and it raged with heat.

"I know you are lurking, planning and plotting."

My only attempt at knowing your location is to blindly grasp for the intruder. My feeble attempt to keep my tormentor from moving, to lessen cancer's attack was useless. The hollow voice of my accuser I could hush; but the battle in my body raged on.

Cries bellowed from every organ in my body. My head now filled with guttural sounds of agony as I attempted to understand if my tormentor had reached the crevices of my brain, to prod on the very essence of who I am.

How, I wished in the darkness I could see what my tormentor planned next. However, I could not.

Every minute mattered in this battle. Every minute. I felt unarmed as this emotionless and strategic tumor continued to gain advantage. Circling around my organs and hunting down his prey.

O' how desperately I wanted to live.

"I want to live!"

Every fiber of my being wanted to fight back.

"If I had a dagger, I would gouge you out myself."

I howled violently in an attempt to be seen and heard by this shrewd terrorist. To my consternation, this predator was emotionless and far too trained to be moved by my weeping. The torture was compounded as I realized no help would reach me,

"Where is my help?"

The tormentor laughingly prodded at me for he was protected by layers of skin, tissues, fat, ligaments and a cruel capitalistic system. Unmoving, completely still as my torture continued. In the darkness, in my aloneness with my sweat and tears;

I acquiesced.

There was no way to block this out, it was with me every second of the day.

One night my tormentor really decided to show me his cruel abuse of power. I attempted to get it out of bed and my body felt unusually heavy. I looked around to see what was holding me down and I was absolutely surrounded by a pool of water. "Did I lose control of my bladder? My entire side was soaked."

My body was freezing and I just felt odd.

I mustered up enough energy to stand up. I stood over my bed and I could see the imprint of my body in the sheets as if I were still in bed.

My head. My back. My arms. My legs were still in perfect form, like a mold created by sand and a wave of my fear. My teeth chattered as a shiver from a cold that iced my bones passed through my soul. "God, what is this?" I touched my hair and the strands felt like a wet mop. Suddenly, the words of my doctor were loud and clear in my head,

"Night sweats will begin because your immune system is

trying to fight something that it cannot win."

"My God, this battle just will not go away! Just Go Away! Present and ready to kill, huh? Gimme a Break!"

The cold began to rise from my toes, through my legs and arms as my face became frozen in terror. My finger-tips became like porcelain and I- I could not move.

Frozen. I stood there bug-eyed and drenched in anxiety as this enemy encroached.

My statue like frame stared at the imprint of my body on my bed. My perception being forced to change. Forced to change.

"What does this mean? Is this cancer moving? Do I need to go to the hospital now? Is it in my brain? Is it in my liver, my bones or my spine?"

The avalanche of thoughts forcefully sloping in my mind came to an abrupt halt as I heard a soft voice, "Mom are you okay?" Jihree entered my seclusion and I couldn't answer him. I could not fake an answer, nor a smile. I was a statue molded by fear and frozen in my reality.

Having no answer; any words I spoke would just be empty. The realization was sinking in that I could not hide this from him, nor myself. This reality was not subtle. This battle I could not ignore.

My hands could not restore this one and no help appeared to be coming.

Gasping for air.

"I just need to catch my breath. I just need a
moment to breathe. I-I-I can-not breathe!"

A shallow breath in warmed my frozen feet and allowed me to move. I ran as fast as I could to leave my place of seclusion, for it no longer sheltered me from this tornado. I slowly glanced at my son as I ran directly into the eye of the storm.

The strength of the wind I carried caused me to crash into the walls as I attempted to make it to my office. The gust of pain shattered the frames and pictures as I ran frantically down the stairs. I missed two-three steps at a time. Pain receptors covered in my adrenaline forced my heart to drum out of my chest. I reached the bottom of my stairs and slid into my office. I hit the floor with a crash of reality.

Aaaaaaaaaaaaaaaaaaaaaaaaaahhhhhhhhhhhhhhhhhhhhh!

An ear-piercing wail came from the depths of my being. My lamentations erupted.

Out came a sound that had nothing to do with my vocal cords, my larynx, nor my articulators.

The sound appeared to be detached from my mouth.

My expressions of grief came from the depths of my inner being. My misunderstanding. My disappointments. My hurt. My despair. My wants. My needs. My anger. My life. My love. The wail was riddled with energy.

My windows quaked.

Once the quivering in the windows and my body stopped. There was a penetrable silence. Once again, slow and deliberate there was that voice again; this time very stern as the silence recognized His power.

"WHO DO YOU SAY THAT I AM?"

Somehow, I knew this moment was imperative.

This moment and question was essential to progressing pass this stint.

The last couple of weeks or maybe even all of my life, I never truly gave real consideration to being in an exact moment. I was always planning for a future or addressing past choices.

"What does it mean to be completely concentrated in this moment?"

Is it even possible to have my awareness fully focused at this present juncture?

For in that hour, I was being asked to summarize my knowledge of God and our relationship in the most detailed verbiage in an attempt to foreshadow my future.

"God, who do I say you are?"

I repeated the question aloud. My negation was no longer effective.

I had to stomach my own truth.

I comprehended my reality and all the factors that would not fade. I continued to contemplate this interval and the probing. I closed my eyes tight in an effort to simply recede. Somehow, still recognizing the importance of this crossroad; I pulled from all the elements of my life.

I gulped in all of my apprehensions, my past mistakes, my past success and my desire for a future.

I absorbed them all inward with an anguished swallow.

I tasted it!

I stayed in that bitter, painful and exhausting moment.

My eyes closed, my body and mind fully engaged.

Gradually. Unhurriedly, I digested the bitterness and sour taste of misunderstanding.

I retorted pushing past all my religious experiences.

My years of attending church and quoting scriptures, with great resistance…it was very difficult for me to answer. I felt in some way my honesty was sacrilegious; however, I pushed through the facade as I answered,

"I personally don't know who you are!"

My pride now on the floor and my physical stature slowly followed. Positioned in my truth as I looked over this dry land. Naked in this wilderness I could see me, me and more me.

My lack of understanding. My illusion of control. My fear. My doubt. My anger. My resentment. My mistrust. Me!

Aspects of me now all stood boldly pointing back from the reflection of my tears.

All at once, I succumbed to my reality. The problems I faced in addition to cancer. The certainty that I could not handle this on my own, nor did I know where to begin.

I blew out from within the depths of my being; the life force I knew and held on to escaped me. My body collapsed on my cold office floor. With that last blow of my own breath …..I surrendered.

I cannot recall how long I stayed on the floor in my office that day. I know I saw the sun come up and I could faintly hear Anthony wrestling with the kids.

I could not stop. I could not leave my office.

I was in the middle of an all-out battle. I was wrestling. I could not stop. I could not have any breaks or interruptions. The sun slowly drew back into the clouds and the moon leisurely took its place.

There I was still naked on the floor.

In this low and narrow place all around me I could clearly see large mountains towering me as I sought to cover my nakedness.

To my dismay, there were many mountains around me. I anticipated the mountain labeled cancer to tower the other peaks. I turned over on my back with my breast facing the emptiness as I pointed to the mountains and labeled as many as I could.

Aloud I pointed and named as many as I willing to see at that juncture:

"There is misunderstanding. There is disbelief. Oh' there is that hurt from my ex-husband, that cut deep. There is the hill of past mistakes; geez, past hurts was about to have a mud slide, while mistrust was full of ice."

Wow, they were all different from the mountain called cancer; however, they were all just as massive.

The very elevation of the mountains made it difficult for me to breathe. The atmosphere was suffocating. The true nature of the mountains caused me to gasp for air. My breathing was laborious making it was impossible for me to speak. Thus, I allowed the cries of my heart to whisper,

"I- I can't breathe. God, I just need you to help me breathe."

As I was attempting to manage my breaths, once again there was that voice. The voice was recognizable and the tone unchanged by my whimpers;

"WHO DO YOU SAY THAT I AM?"

In the depths of my suffering. In the hollowness, the emptiness, and the brokenness; I attempted to search my ideals of God.

My traditions framed through childhood. My teen years spent on the choir. My every Sunday spent at church; I pulled from all of those moments in an attempt to answer my understanding of God.

In the bareness of my honesty;

"God, I realize my understanding of you was always given to me through the perception or ideals of others. My life was consumed with keeping traditional patterns, regurgitating words and scriptures without having understanding."

Now facing a limitation in my seconds, minutes and hours.

"I wish I would have used my time more wisely."

Through my sobbing I managed to utter,

"Well, God it could not have all been in vain, for

Somehow, in this valley I hear you now."

Recognizing my error and my mistake in using the church as a crutch, always looking to be fed instead of seeking you for myself. I simply closed my eyes,

"I missed it, but now I am aware. I know you are real and I ask you to forgive me for missing it. Let's begin."

I was able to leave my office floor. I made my way upstairs. Jihree, Jelani and Anthony now asleep and unaware of this transitional plane I was entering.

I climbed into my bed; however, this time my cogitation concentrated on my knowledge of God as I contemplated the question,

"WHO DO YOU SAY THAT I AM?"

Until I closed my eyes for sleep. I turned to my alarm clock with eagerness. I set my alarm for 3:00 a.m.

My 3:00 a.m. time arrived and nothing magical happened throughout the night.

My side of the bed was still soaked from my night sweats. My hair no longer needed any heat, it would no longer stay straight due to the sweat that would run from my scalp, to my neck and down my back.

The mass still protruded from my left breast and my lymph nodes now swollen, palpable and spongy.

My physical condition unchanged during my hours of pondering about my knowledge of God. I didn't bother to change my wet clothes or tieback my mini afro before going to my office for prayer. Once there I closed the door and decided to begin simply with music.

The melody from the piano echoed slowly around the four corners of the room. The beautiful sound of a tenor followed the piano:

Here is my heart, I give it lord to you

Here is my life, I lay it before you

Where else would I go?

What else would I do?

If I did not know you?

How deeply I need you

How deeply I need you, my lord

How deeply I need you, my lord

Like the desert needs the rain, I need you

Like the ocean needs the streams, I need you

Like the morning needs the sun, I need you

Lord you are my only one

In every way, and every day

I need you"*

   *How Deeply I Need You, Shekinah Glory. 2004

The sweet sounds of exhortation truly embodied everything I felt and needed to say in that moment. Once the sound of the soloist and the choir stopped singing. Somehow, through the traps and snares placed on me by the rumination in my own mind. My strained and tearful voice could now be heard. Progressively moving beyond the story being played over and over in my head; my low and meek voice slowly began to gain volume.

I begin to repeat the chorus over and over. When the song was over, I would sing it again. And Again. And Again. I had to sing pass my desires to understand the why's, how's and what was to happen next. For in that moment it was out of my control. Resistance traveled from my toes, crept up my limbs and passed through the center of my being.

The opposition caused my stomach to turn in knots.

As my reluctance passed my stomach, there was a tightness in my chest and next my jaws locked.

This place in my life caused much turmoil…I knew I could not stay there.

"I can't stay here."

I was at a crossroad. The battle between the two planes was palpable.

My spirit desired to rise above my panoply of flesh comprised of my stubbornness, my pride, my selfishness and my desire to allow my emotions to rule my every action.

In the dwelling of these two planes, slowly I could see my skin falling to the ground around me.

As, I continued to acknowledge my errors, my skin began to fall in layers like soft-serve ice cream.

The tightness slowly released its stronghold as I freed my plans to climb, scratch, or claw my way out of my trapped space. I accepted my ideas for escape would all fail me and with no help coming from the outside world.

I curled inward. I curled inward.

"In him I live and have my being."

I curled inward.

"Lord you are Lord. You are King of Kings. Your mercy and love endures forever. Thank you for your grace and your loving kindness. Your forgiveness. Your everlasting love is never changing. There is no one like you. Thank you for extending your love and your grace. Your grace and mercy is better than LIFE itself. Lord your thoughts of me are beautiful. I worship you just for who you are; you are everything, everything to me. I acknowledge your presence. I need your presence. Lord, you are sovereign in all your ways. I love you, Lord. I don't understand all, but I do know you are worthy of all honor and all praise. Your ways are higher than mine. My desire is to have understanding of your ways and know who you are personally. Thank you Lord. You will forever be my strength, my hope, my redeemer."

I found myself on my knees, however this time not from the heaviness I carried on my neck piled on by the shackles on my mind. On my knees in this place I knelt near an altar, however, not an altar in a man-made building.

This altar was seen when I closed my eyes and searched my ideals. This altar was within.

The power of this place forced me to an all four position with my hands and knees clinging to the floor. Recognizing, although this altar felt very personal I was not alone in this place.

"Holy, Holy. Holy, Holy!" A mercy seat was created.

I presented no request, no pleas, and no demands. The gentleness and the sweetness of this place made Time stand still. Time was finally quiet in the tranquility.

After moments of true worship: my spirit, my mind and my voice fully engaged. The outward distractions now appeared as background noise, for my face stayed on what was in front of me.

I relinquished any desires of my own.

My encounter was empowering. I was reminded of God's presence. My thirst for intimacy forced me to face my comprehension. I probingly asked,

"God, I know you are real and your word never changes; what am I missing? I recognize I am the problem here; your word changes not, help me understand. I desire understanding. Help me understand."

After my question I sat completely still. The atmosphere was filled with a remarkable quietness; the quiet was uncanny; however, not frightening. I felt no need to hasten this silence... to my surprise I loitered in the tranquility. I embraced this silence. The suffocating walls of my blue office became porous allowing air to pass. I was no longer fixated on the tumor on my left breast, nor the thoughts of my death.

Preoccupation of my kid's future without me, halted.

I stayed in this place. I spoke no words, yet I knew everything I wanted to say was heard. He heard my cries.

In the presence every inch of me called upon his name.

The pull was innate as if I knew this place before birth. I curled inward.

I gazed into the silence after worship. Unexpectedly, out of this silence came a sound, however, not from an outward source. At this particular point, I was unaware of where the sound emanated. Deliberately and penetrating, I heard the words;

"Genesis, start there."

Quickly, I open my eyes and looked to the left and to the right. I looked behind me and no one was present. I looked down and the only person visible was my own reflection in my tear drops.

The sun was beginning to rise, but without resistance or hesitation on my part; I grabbed my Bible. I felt like a child on Christmas day. My excitement began to take over my body and emotions.

Outwardly, I wanted to jump up and down in an attempt to release all the feelings going on inside.

I pushed passed all the demands on my desk.

The data I collected from cancer organizations and all my denial letters for help, included in the stack were the letters to my children.

One swoosh from my hand, the papers took on feather-like qualities, as they slowly floated through the air and rhythmically one by one landed on the cold floor.
The clutter and noise now removed.
I made space for the new. I made space for the new.

I excitedly slammed my bible on my desk, like I had the winning domino in hand. I opened Genesis and simply stated, "Show me."

There I sat and began with: "In the beginning."

I sat and read: the creation, Adam and Eve, Noah, Cain and Abel, Abraham, Lot, Abimelech, Jacob, and Joseph. There I physically sat in my chair at my desk for hours and hours.

I searched the words in Genesis as if were looking for a treasure, a mystery, a quest.

I stood on my tiptoes to look on a high shelf. I crawled below rocks and knelt down between tiny crevices as I continued my search. To my surprise, I was no longer searching for scriptures pertaining to healing as I tried hours, days and weeks prior. The deep penetrating voice I heard now captured my mind. I was attempting to read until I heard that voice speak again.

Day in…Day out I read.

Genesis stayed with me long into the mid-day and into the night. Throughout the next couple of days I waited for return calls from my insurance company to tell me,

"We made a mistake!" Never happened.

The cancer organizations did not return calls with any magical news. The large cancerous tumor, still very visible and making itself known. With all the uncertainty around me, I knew within I was given a task and there I stayed in Genesis.

In Genesis, I stayed.

My 3:00 a.m. prayer time was where I started; however, my time seeking did not stop throughout the day. I carried Genesis in the kitchen, in the bathroom and my bedroom. Each morning, my prayer time would begin with worship, praise and then a stillness.

I would continue in Genesis. Continue in Genesis. Continue in Genesis.

The next morning and the next 3:00 a.m. time would arrive and I continued with the same routine until I proudly reached the end of Genesis.

"I was waiting with earnest expectation. What is next? Lord, what is next?"

I allowed myself to rest in the inner tranquility and during the stillness after worship, I listened and there it was again. Oh' how excited I was to hear more direction; my ears and heart heightened,

"Yes, what is my next move?"

The voice simply stated, "Read it again!" I quickly replied,

"Read Genesis again! Read Genesis Again?"

Without hesitation I began in the beginning again.

In Genesis, I stayed.

Consistently, I searched high and low with my heart and my mind concentrating on what I was reading. I read, read and read without mention of cancer, nor my fate. Slowly and intentionally, I began to read for understanding. Certain questions began to stick out in my mind.

"Jacob's name was changed to Israel, after he wrestled …but there were certain times when you still referred to him as Jacob."

I was beginning to process what I was reading.

"I don't want to memorize it, I want to know and understand."

One morning after reading I naturally entered a place of worship. My worship was becoming very intimate. Out of the natural flow of my understanding. The shift in my thoughts were now expressed through my mouth.

I no longer made foreign repetitions I once heard the mothers of the church shout.

I now wanted God to hear me.

I wanted my adoration to kiss his cheeks and touch his ears. I wanted him to know my mind, my spirit, my voice and my heart was now occupied with praise for him.

Eyes closed. Truth took shape as I whispered into the ears of my creator, which spoke this world into existence. Out of my spirit, I began to bless his name. No yelling, No sputtering. My voice spoke like soft cotton as our intimacy ascended to new heights.

I wanted him to know and understand how I was beginning to feel about my One, True God. Through growth and understanding, my many gods were recognized. I was surpassing this dry and barren land seen with my natural eyes. I worshiped in truth.

"O, the heavens tell how great you are, the earth is full of your goodness. How powerful and majestic you are."

To my natural eyes this place was unfathomable; sight used beyond my sensual perception I could see myself whispering with my spirit as I spoke to my creator. Our intimacy always included welcoming an amazing stillness. The stillness was not comprised of Time. Absolutely everything stood still in the power of HIS presence.

I ambled in the tranquility of this silence. The tranquility appeared to stretch to eternity. In this amazing hush, I once again heard the voice.

This time the words where accompanied with images, images and more images.

The voice felt very near now, as if it was coming from within. Repeatedly I heard,

"I need this to be seen. I need this to be seen!"

As the images flashed before me, I watched the images closely and attempted to make sense of them as they flashed quickly, "Jesus! What are you saying? What are you showing me?"

In my stillness, slowly out of the pure silence, the sounds of rushing wind engulfed me. I gazed around at the pureness and with a powerful gust of air a large bloodshot veil masked my view.

"I can't see the light and the gentle blows of wind anymore."

The veil was so near to my face, the line of demarcation between my skin and the veil was undetectable. The veil was impenetrable and concealed all of the light that was once present in my serenity. The illumination in my silence was now diminished. I remained unafraid.

Beyond my innate senses. My desire for understanding was developing an appetite. A hunger. A thirst.

My proclivity to jump ahead had to be contained. Inside my desire to understand wanted to move faster than the images being presented. My great need for interpretation was bouncing up and down from within.

My yearning was budding as I continued to look beyond my physical eyes.

Swiftly, a loud thunderous reverberation surrounded me and I spun around in a circle chasing the echoes. The noise was filled with the sounds of a thousand crashing mirrors as the veil shattered in a hollow place.

The veil collapsed with such power causing every inch of me to awaken.

My hunger and anticipation amplified. My thoughts swirled in my head like fudge being stirred in vanilla ice cream.

"God, why did it shatter? The veil was rent from top to bottom at the crucifixion…why are you showing me this? What was to be revealed?"

Before I could grasp the meaning, instantly I was standing among family members and friends.

"Hey Mom. Hey Jihree. Hey Cousin Sherika and Bridgette. Hey Dad and William….Humm, I don't know you or you." I smiled as I attempted to recognize all of the faces there in the crowd.

My smile quickly turned to bewilderment as I clearly heard,

"I need them to see this! I need this to be seen!"

Abruptly, my excitement was placed on hold as my physical senses heightened and dread began to leave an impression.

"Lord, my place of vulnerability and possibly the process of my death. Lord, you want me to call and include all those people? Lord, my son to watch his mother endure this process?"

I agonized with what I was seeing with my natural eyes; I could not understand. I continued to look intently at a person standing in the middle of a large crowd.

I could not see the person's face. I walked all around curiously trying to recognize the person, for the person felt familiar.

Lives were being touched and changed as God used this person. My anxiety was calmed as I could see this person touching many lives. My apprehension turned to joy and my pain turned to purpose as I once again heard,

"I need this to be seen."

Outwardly tears flowed. Inwardly, I was back at an altar. The wrestling and tussling could be felt at the core of my being. My insides flipped and flopped.

I presented my bargaining,

"Jesus, I know you can heal me. I really, really believe you can heal me in an instance…. Didn't you say by your strips we were…?"

I suddenly stopped talking for in that moment my redundancy spoke volumes.

I once again realized my errors. My bargaining was not filled with understanding.

"Lord, I realize that if I had real understanding and knew how to stand on truth; I would not need to bargain with the creator of heaven and earth."

My head shook shamefully to the left and to the right in disappointment with myself as I self-confessed:

"Allissen your pleas are curtailed by your endeavor to manipulate and not transform. Transformation. Be transformed by the renewing of your mind."

Curling inward, I marched right back to that altar. Within, I allowed the higher things of God to take precedent. My lower levels of understanding and concerns of myself were recognized. My outward flesh trembled and cried out,

"Let this pass me!"

However, beyond my sensual perception…I knew this was essential.

Hovering in this plane of two realms. I accepted purpose needed to manifest into my physical realm.

Purpose was attempting to engulf me like a rushing river.

"Oh' just allow the river to flow, Allissen."

The river felt mighty and intimidating, yet on some level felt innate. My nakedness in the river would cause more coldness and bruising.

My skin desired to avoid any more pain. Looking at the water parallel to this dry valley, something inside of me yearned for the river.

The towering mountains in this valley plummeted rocks. I scrambled to hold on to the remnants. In this plane my hands were unwilling to release my tight grip on the vestiges; nevertheless, something intrinsic was drawing me to the river. The river current was strong and the pull on me was great.

I timidly released my grip on my ideals. I emancipated my fingers nervously… one at a time. One finger at a time, I released my hold. A blow from a gentle wind and my body was in the water.

"Lord, I am in the water and this river is stirring. I
thought this would be refreshing? "
The coldness and intense currents on my bare skin did not permeate through my anxiety, nor my desire to dictate my direction for my own life.
"Curl inward, Allissen."

As, I slowly released my desire to control the elements in the river and the speed of the flow. Once, I acknowledged who was in control of the river, to my surprise the roaring rapids calmed its tone.

My feather-like being whisked about in the water.
The sweet perfume of tranquility forced me to open my eyes. Once opened, the strength in the rays of light pierced through

the mountains causing the water to illuminate.

Sparkles of gold flakes and diamonds danced around in the water. The river was enticing. Deliberately, I opened my mouth and sipped.

The water was refreshing. The taste was sweet and stayed on my lips like honey. I whirled around in the water as it continued to rise in this valley. The water continued to rise as I let go. I let go.

The water continued to rise. The water continued to rise.

The water reached a certain level and then poured over.

The river tipped over with me in its gentle currents.

The bucketing instantly overflowed and I was back on my office floor.

I was back on my office floor facing Genesis.

The river freed me back at the beginning.

I could still taste the sweetness on my lips as I looked upon Genesis. The taste reminded me of my next task. I sat and decided on the best way to communicate to everyone in my vision. I typed a long email and I detailed the veil, the lives and the ministry. I wrote down every detail that was displayed in the images. Every detail as it was revealed to me, even bits I did not fully comprehend at that intersection. I even excitedly typed, "Someone is going to touch many lives and bring many to know the love of God."

Email allowed everyone to hear it from my mouth describing the images shown to me in my vision. I prepared the email and restrained my hesitation. I spoke gently in prayer as certain facts drilled in through my church attendance stuck out:

"God, what about life and death being in the power of the tongue?" Everyone is not going to speak well of this matter! Are we creating a bigger battle? God, am I placing myself in a situation where I am going to have to battle everyone's fears plus my own?"

I pushed through all my apprehensions and vulnerability. I followed the instructions given to me with one tap on the 'enter' button. Once I hit send, I instantly heard the voice,

"Most cannot speak things into their own life, let alone yours. Whose voice do you reverence more?"

I chuckled like a child, for I asked a question and this time God quickly responded.

The Living Word and my understanding collided. Took shape. The words could be seen like particles floating in the air making the words alive;

"Draw nigh to me and I will draw nigh unto you."

I endeavored to stay in this place of tranquility; however, the background noise was now filled with the sounds of my telephone.

Ring! Ring! Ring! Ring! Ring! R-I-N-G! RING! RING RING! "Here We Go!"

Phone call after phone call. Email after email.

"Here we go!"

There were tears, tears, tons of questions, and critiques.
Yes, critiques.

"How did this happen to you? You never drank or smoked…you are the good one! Why you?"

"Allissen you know the veil was rent from top to bottom with Christ."

"Some of your biblical understanding is incorrect."

"I want you to say this scripture every day."

"Are you still living with Anthony? How old is your baby?"

"Here is a number to a prayer line."

"Here is Benny Hinn's schedule."

"Come to this miracle service."

"This church is having a healing service on this day."

"Curse without cause would not come."

"Parents ate sour grapes and the children's teeth are set on edge."

"The word of the Lord wanted me to tell you…"

The biblically astute phone calls became very critical for my further ascent; my biblical understanding was critiqued so heavily.

I would answer as many calls as I could stand in one day and then I would quit. I had to shut-up all that noise.

As I truly began to process the responses to my news. The understanding of everyone could be seen like a road map. Their responses were built on landmarks labeled: cliché's, traditions, redundancy and regurgitations. Their reactions were mimicked. I sat puzzled at most responses.

"God is that real understanding?"

My retort to everyone's critiques, comments, and gossip actually surprised me. I did not feel the need to answer their questions or reply to their judgements. HUSH!

Slowly, the fallacies in our understanding or misunderstandings bounced around the corners of the room as if in a pin-ball machine.

I stood in the center analyzing the perception of others. The comments spoken from the outside world could have led me in several directions. I could have journeyed back down the road of condemnation holding on to the hand that asked

"Why you?"

The questions regarding my biblical understanding could have caused me to retreat from seeking my own understanding. To lean back on accepting someone else's knowledge of God, which extended from their biases-successes and failures. However, I knew I was in the presence of God.

We were just beginning our very intimate dialogue, and the spirit of truth would reveal the meanings.

The meaning of the veil sitting on my face like skin. The veil then being torn with the sound of glass would soon be revealed. The questions and conversations created a greater hunger and intensity to go deeper in his presence. Transformation was happening before my eyes. It was real.

I was no longer moved by the swirls of the wind blowing in uncontrolled cyclic motions for the boat was beginning to steady. The anchor was becoming visible.

My physical world still resembled the view I had seen as I cowered in the corner of my blue office.

The look of concern on my eldest son's face had not changed, the look of defeat on my Anthony's face was still present. Nevertheless, my perception of my physical world was shifting. My face was changing. Eyes closed and in the darkness I was no longer fixated on whether the cancer was moving or if the tumor was becoming larger and more lymph nodes swollen. My notes to self, stopped:

"Allissen stay off your left side, don't put pressure on the tumor, maybe this will help contain it in the breast."

My mind was now busying itself with things from above. I loved our time of worship. I was committing all that I was and he was drawing me near. I begin to worship him and only him. I no longer worshipped a life I once knew.

One night with Anthony to my right, my baby in the middle and Jihree across my feet. I could hear a song rising from my inner being. All of my physical matter had surrendered. In my continuous place of yielding; I extended my right arm. I defied the tightness and swelling of my left arm as I lifted it as high as I could.

Complete preoccupation with my own hopes, fears, and plans were diminishing. Unhurriedly, in my head a piano played, a bass guitar, and then the strings of a violin played. Out of my mouth, the most powerful instrument caroled:
"For Thou O' Lord art high above all thee earth;
thou art exalted far above, O-O, God
Thou O' Lord art high above all the earth
 thou art exalted far above, O-O-O, God
I exalt thee, I exalt thee, I exalt thee, O-O-O, Lord.
I exalt thee, I exalt thee, I exalt thee, O-O-O, Lord.
I exalt thee, I exalt thee, I exalt thee, O-O-O, Lord.
I love you lord and I lift my voice to worship you, O' my soul rejoices; take joy my king in what you hear, let it be a sweet, sweet sound in your ear."

As my gratitude, love, and new thoughts continued to flow from the outer portion of my mind; the tears streamed any resistance I still carried from my eyes.

Right then. Right there. Right then. Right there.
The atmosphere changed.

The matters of this world were cloaked. No longer could I see my attempts at tranquility. My material possessions. My attachments to this world all dissipated in the glory of his presence.

I entered true tranquility. My heart longed for Him. I opened my eyes and I could see HIS presence was EVERYWHERE.

Tangible. Perceptible. Powerful. Illuminating.

I closed my eyes for sleep with more questions dancing around in my head. I wanted more. 3:00 a.m. time and my alarm clock was no longer needed. The gentle voice of my Heavenly Father within would nudge me, I was eager to sit at his table to eat of the manna presented.

The word had become my daily bread.

"You are my daily bread."

We laughed. We talked. He questioned my understanding in order to tear down my erring beliefs. I welcomed his chastisement for I could now feel the time spent in this place was enjoyed by us both. He longed for me to enter his presence, just as much as I wanted to be there. I began to cherish the temple and the presence that filled each crevice with a sweet fragrance. I chased his presence, for I never wanted to be far away.

In praise and worship I wanted my worship to reach him, to touch him. Once my adoration reached him, I made room. I made room. I waited in the silence. I was overwhelmed with kindness as my heart longed for his presence. My heart longed for him. I knew he was waiting on me and had been there waiting.

"You were waiting on me."

O' how excited I was to know that he inhabits my praises. Once my acclaim pushed through the courts; no skin, no scars, no separation. Just truth and freedom. I was aware, fully aware of HIS presence. Transformation was happening as the Spirit descended like rain.

Every layer of my skin dissolved like sugar as the rain poured.

On one particular morning at 3:00 a.m. I closed my eyes tight blocking all outward issues.

"Keep your eyes on Him."

I allowed the water to rise. The water poured from a cloud covering my home and I could hear water flowing beneath me. The taste of replenishing forced me to kneel. As I knelt, a well was formed; the rain water now poured into the well. I began to drink from the rain water that fell into that well. As I continued to drink, I could hear the roars of water moving. The water was rushing with great force. I knew something was being birthed.

Eagerly, I grabbed on to the sides of this well with my hands as I continued to exclaim my new understandings. The rushing water made the sound of thunder. The sounds did not alarm me; I had to force myself to wait on the water. The waters continued to rise and rise.

Intrinsically, my hands released the sides of the well. I extended my arms into the air like wings in anticipation of the fresh water. The sound of thunder engulfed me as one huge wave burst through my walls and engulfed the temple.

My eyes now fixated on the water, as I spun in its power. Slowly, slowly out of each ripple of water, letters and more letters formed. Next words took shape. The words swam around me and spun with great force. From the river the words took shape:

"And by the river upon the bank thereof, on this side and on that side, shall grow all trees for meat, whose leaf shall not fade, neither shall the fruit thereof be consumed: it shall bring forth new fruit according to his months, because their waters they issued out of the sanctuary: and the fruit thereof shall be for meat, and the leaf thereof for medicine."

The atoms and electrons began to circulate in rhythm. The forced gained momentum filling the space as the energy and the life in every word bellowed through the temple.

My heart thumped loud and intensely as I whirled in this vortex of energy. The water percolated through my pores by osmosis, as I coiled in the words. My body now porous as I absorbed the words.

In the distance, the background noise in my home could faintly be heard.

Ring-Ring-Ring-Ring!

However, it could not penetrate, for my roots were deepening. Nothing could remove me from this place. The words were providing nutrition while the water helped the sustenance seep into the ground.

My prior minutes, hours and days spent searching to know him and simply just to know him were manifesting.

In one drink I was filled from my head to my toes. As I sat with my creator in the middle of this monsoon that now covered my dry lands. I could truly grasp that he was my God.

In the downpour my Heavenly Father knew what I was in need of without me asking. My pleas were no longer needed as I continued to simply make room. Simply make room. Open the door. Open the door.

I soaked up every drop of the water and decided complete understanding was necessary. Worldly interpretation of the word would return void.

I craved spiritual understanding to make the word tangible in my physical world. Customary practices and this outward religion I had seen throughout my life would tell me:

"Learn the scripture, memorize it, and write it down on index cards, confess it, confess it, let's see if you can say it by memory, and believe it."

The words was describing real transformation and how real transformation must come. I longed for truth and to know understanding. I wanted to know how to apply understanding to my life.

My physical world needed to mirror what was going on spiritually. In order to have true belief, I needed to understand. I began to speak the words repeatedly and I asked,

"God, now if I repeat it enough, does that equate to belief?"

In awareness I blurted, "Errors!"

A mirror was beginning to take shape before my eyes. In my reflection, I could see myself attempting to stand on a crate. My first attempt, I simply stood the wood crate upright. After making sure it was straight I forcefully took both legs and stood on the crate. As I attempt to remain upright and vertical, I had to use my own body weight to remain balanced. Eventually, the crate gives under my pressure.

Next, I could see myself grabbing a wood crate for

inspection. I look to see what the crate is made of and I attempt to understand how and why the crate was created. I turn the crate vertical and then horizontal as I determine the way the crate was designed to be stood on. After taking some time to understand its design and how to make use of the design properly. I gracefully stand on the crate with my full body. Standing on the crate was now done with more ease after understanding the crate's design and purpose.

The mirror in which I was learning my own face truly empowered. I wanted to take immediate action. I felt as if should be doing something now, in my day-to-day life.

"How can I improve my prayer life further? Maybe my diet, 'leaves for healing'… Maybe I can start with my eating habits."

I researched cancer and diet and tons of information filled the screen. I snickered as I attempted to process all of the information.

"Okay Lord, is broccoli, kale, blueberries, apricot seeds, tomatoes and baking soda my new diet?"

I smiled as I waited in the silence, for I knew this time I would not receive a response. There was a pull on me to wait, to simply remain still.

In the stillness, I pondered on my readings of Genesis and the several references to trees and water. I also thought about the mist that covered the earth in Genesis, "was that confusion?"

> *"And out of the ground made the Lord God to grow every tree that is pleasant to the sight, and good for food; the tree of life also in the midst of the garden, and the tree of knowledge of good and evil."*

After my ponderings and recalling of the impetuous but controlled flow of water and the power and energy the water possessed. I closed my eyes and visualized the crucifixion as the blood and water gushed from the side of Jesus as the spear pierced through his side.

I mused on this day and night. Day and night.

> *"But one of the soldiers with a spear pierced his side, and immediately came there out blood and water."*

In my day-to-day world, the telephone rings and the pop-ups at my home continued consistently. The draining calls full of me listening to the outside world attempt to ask their questions with delicacy, as they pushed through the difficulty of framing it all to make sense.

After my denials for Benny Hinn's schedule and my unwillingness to grasp their understanding of the veil. People would begin to approach me in a half-hesitant sort of way; they eyed my curiously, compassionately, and with pity, all in one glance. I knew I had to remain rooted and I did not feel an urge to move from this intimate place of worship. My new place of worship equipped me with learning to silence the background noise. I could simply turn and gesture,

"SSSSHHHHHHH! Hush," as the background noise struggled to affect my sensual perception.

One day as I was enjoying my new roots, I sat in my office and I stared out of my window looking at two generations. From the window in blue office I could see the children outside playing with bikes, balls and their family dogs. I enjoyed the smiles and their laughter in this vast space.

I secretly placed myself as a transparent companion as we discussed what game to play next.

"Do you want to play dodge ball next or hopscotch?" I watched as they ran up and down the street chasing sticks and balls, tirelessly.

"Did we ever get tired when we played outside from sun up to sun down?" I gawked contently out of my window at the gaps in time.

RINNNNNGGGGG!!!

A loud ring from the background noise startled me from my nostalgic state. I glanced at my phone and a familiar face flashed with each ring.

I snorted for this person had remained very quiet after the news broke. Her call intrigued me. Her voice had remained quiet inside the calamity.

My future Mother-in law is the younger of two children. Born in Selma, Alabama. She walked with Dr. King during the Civil Rights Movement. I reflected on her life as her picture flashed with each ring.

Momma Jones' skin tone was shining bronze, her black hair never out of place. Her black almond shaped eyes were stern; however, framed by a kind face. Her impression was always one of infinite patience, but unstoppable determination. I would later come to know the softness of her bosom. With a curious apprehension I answered, "Hello, Mrs. Jones." I welcomed her curious silence versus all the chatter of hypocrisy, fear, and doubt after my announcement.

Her tone and confidence always demanded the noise to stop. By nature and profession, she was steady and stern. Cloaked under her stern demeanor, a passionate voice spoke clearly and deliberately. No pretense given, No hellos just:

"Allissen, I have been in prayer, God wanted me to give you a number. Get a pen and paper. I will wait. ......Now, his name is Wayne and he is a Biochemist. He works with natural healing and diet. Call him immediately. I have known him for years and I work with him regarding all natural remedies, Call Him!" Mrs. Jones stated in her direct tone.

Out the shadow of nostalgia, my full attention was magnetized to her every word. Her speech was not cliché; it was not out of redundant patterns. The span of time she spent in her silence before opening her mouth spoke volumes to my soul. Her motives were not full of wanting to be heard. In the last hours and days since my life changed; I knew she allowed her world to be changed as well.

Her voice now filled with his presence and out of understanding came agreement. Out of understanding came agreement.

Recognizing higher versus lower levels of understanding and reacting, I humbly and meekly bowed in obeisance.

The picture of a beautiful woman kissed by the sun, now glistened. Purpose and hope was interconnected and interdependent. "Thank you Mrs. Jones, I will call him immediately." Yes, a systemic love was felt as we hung up and continued in his presence. I shouted,

"Thank you, Jesus," as I twirled in my chair.

Once the conversation with my future Mother-in-law ended, I grabbed my pathology report and thought of everything I wanted to say or ask. Did I know enough about what was really going on to discuss the matter with a scientist? Oh' I did not care at that point if I sounded like a babbling fool; I just longed for more understanding. I dialed the number. Quickly, I hit the send button. I could not understand my nervousness and with each ring my anticipation continued to rise.

Ring-Ring-Ring-Ring-Ring.

By the third ring, O' how I wished he would just answer the telephone. I was not hanging up. The line was just going to ring. "Oh, answer the phone!"

He must have felt my hunger after the fourteenth ring. Finally, he answered. A little squeaky voice answered and I introduced myself. Quickly the squeaky voice interrupted me:

"Little girl, I want to talk to you; however, I need you to call me at 7:30 a.m. tomorrow morning." I quickly replied, "Yes, sir!"

During the night I prepared for my 7:30 a.m. conversation with Wayne, the Biochemist. I studied breast cancer and looked up the meanings to words that I did not understand, nor knew how to pronounce. My notepad was full of questions, definitions, and statistical data. I wrote the types of chemotherapy I needed and how many rounds. After collecting tons of data, I processed the information and once I felt comfortable. I enjoyed the stillness once again and then closed my eyes for sleep.

7:28 a.m. I sat at my glass desk. I could see my reflection slightly between my notes, notepad, pathology report, pens and anxiousness. I dialed the number and exhaled with each ring. To my disappointment there was no answer. The air deflated from my cheeks as I continued to sit with my research and part of my reflection. The noise in my head tuned up,

> "Maybe, I should not call him back. Maybe, I will just call him tomorrow."

I decided to push through the noise, in which my emotions were speaking louder than my desire for understanding. I quickly turned on my praise music and decided to fill my head and the room with the sounds of praise.

8:01 a.m. I gave it at least thirty minutes before calling him back and this time that nasally voice answered. He answered!

"Hello, Little Girl!"

I was thirty-one at this time, but I gladly ignored the creepy 'little girl' comments. Before he could open his mouth to say good morning or ask me my real name… I started my babble. The words ran out of my mouth non-stop. We were both talking at the same time, until one question he asked me stopped me, "Tell me one thing little girl; "What did you eat today?" His question threw me for I was not prepared to discuss breakfast. I stuttered my answer,

"Oat..meal and so...me... juice."

He proceeded to ask me,

"How did you get here, little girl?"

My mouth was now shut as my mind engaged the conversation. I wanted to understand what he was asking. I knew his questions were not to provoke a guilt trip.

He spoke and slowly an introspective process about my life was presented to gain understanding, but not condemnation.

"Little girl tell me what you ate yesterday. Also, how many hours of sleep did you get last night."

asked Wayne the Biochemist.

Me and my wry sense of humor blurted,

"With a cancer in my body that I cannot see...ha-ha, not very much sleep!"

His response was unexpected as he laughed the most awkward, loud and squeaky laugh. The laugh was so loud, I had to pull the phone away from my ear. Through the screeches in his laugh the ice broke and my nervousness eased and the space between us minimized...we just simply began to talk.

We talked, talked, and talked.

Something about his questions...hum. As he spoke I could see myself working two jobs and staying up all night enjoying my 'me- time'. I thought about my fast food daily must haves and the mounds of daily stress in my life. Awareness was growing and I welcomed the growing pains.

I understood his tactics as he talked, for he would ask me a question and not allow space in the conversation for me to answer aloud.

Wayne, really did not seek answers to the questions he was rambling off.

He was subtly accomplishing his goal. Forcing me to look at my behavior.

There were several Selah moments.

Wayne, the biochemist stayed with me for hours on the phone. He explained the increasing prevalence of cancer after the Industrial Revolution. He explained the purpose of the immune system and how our bodies can prevent and fight off cancer cells daily. His questions and conversation provoked more questions regarding the living word I just experienced. Ezekiel 47:12 was becoming part of my understanding. Our conversation surpassed our cell-phones. Although, I had never seen him with my natural eyes, I felt as if I knew him as a great teacher. I lightheartedly accepted my new name, 'Little Girl'.

In the hierarchy of this space he was being used as a great teacher. I was the grass-hopper and he was my Sensei. I closed my eyes as he spoke and listened with my heartbeat. As I tried to get the image of Yoda out of my head, while listening to his voice. Eyes closed, heart open; You change.

As I followed the rhythm of the beat, the melody of my life could be perceived. I took a healthy listen as I glared into my reflection.

During the last couple of weeks, I began true transformation in the spiritual and it was beginning to manifest in my physical world. Wayne, the Biochemist continued to talk and my mind images moved in a circular motion.

I watched a Ferris-wheel of images go around and around as Wayne the biochemist asked,

"Are you serious about change?"

I paused only for a quick second. During the pause, flashes of my latest experiences circled in front of me on this Ferris-wheel. Around and around in front of me the carts circled in front of me one by one.

On the first white cart I could see myself at my internal altar. On the second greyish cart I peeked over into the cart and I could see myself hiding from my kids and myself.

The next cart was crimson. I looked inside and I was surrounded by large overbearing mountains. The last cart was transparent. I could clearly see myself floating in the river after letting go of the pieces of the broken mountains.

Through the mental images appeared my will, emotions, fears and hopes. I could perceive that my weeks during praise, worship, reading, and silence were about to take shape... mold into this physical world. I knew this would require a continued level of commitment; however, I knew now I was on the right wheel. I committedly and emphatically declared,

"Yes! I am ready!"

Phase 2:

ACENSION

The act of rising higher

A significant shift occurs when we start to question and break down preconditioned thoughts, redundant responses, and auto-pilot actions. Allissen C. Jones

The shift to seek understanding as a
NECESSARY foundation will lead to freedom which is a reward of truth.

Be ye transformed by the renewing of your
 mind

And behold, the veil of the temple was rent in twain from the top to bottom; and the earth did quake, and the rocks rent

Veils

As Wayne, the Biochemist and I continued to discuss cancer and what my next steps should include he began to break down my nutritional guide. He continued to call me 'little girl' but I did not mind. We laughed, we talked, he asked questions to provoke thought; he did not wait on answer. His questions were rhetorical in nature. He began to explain to me that my new way of life would include eating seven times per day, consuming only vegetables and a small amount of protein. He described my plate as having 25% of a protein item and 75% vegetables. The vegetables were to be as raw as possible or lightly steamed. Each morning I needed to begin with fruit and throughout the day I needed to consume at least a pound of fruit per day. White sugar was out of the question. Water and 100% juice was all I could drink. Juice from concentrate was full of sugar. As Wayne, the Biochemist spoke, I took the most detailed notes.

Wayne would mention the food item and then educated me on the role it played in my body.

Wayne would go further and require ten hours of sleep per night each day as I healed. He explained the role of sleep, my immune system and my digestive system in fighting off illness.

As he continued to speak, my mind images continued and I took some steps back and in the steps I could see myself working two jobs, stopping for fast food for lunch, and then staying up nightly until my eyes gave in to sleep. As we continued to talk for hours and hours, the bright blue color in my office was now visible.

The thick haze resting in the room was disintegrating. In the murkiness I could see the haze was made of small particles of misunderstanding, fear, ignorance, victimization, and powerlessness. The mist had become less dense allowing more information to diffuse through the room. As the cloak of fog lifted I looked down on my glass desk and there in the glass I caught a glimpse of my eyes.

As I looked into my eyes, I took a healthy glimpse at my life and my choices over the past couple of years. The questions from Wayne, the Biochemist, did not invoke condemnation, but this time a true look at my behavior and beliefs. The questions were both probing and empowering at the same time. We concluded our conversation with a list of herbs I needed to begin and he gave me specific times to take each vitamin and herb.

Before saying goodbye, he emphasized, "No Cow milk!" I acknowledged his last comment and expressed my gratitude. In one conversation I gained more information from him than from all the doctor's I met with previously. Once I ended the call, I sat in the room to absorb all the information.

With the fog now diminishing in this new place. The sun rays pierced through my blinds and impressed upon my face; my teeth sparkled as I wedged my face deeper in the intensity of the light.

My flat and withdrawn complexion now felt golden. A smile that extended from my new roots was now visible. Sharply impaled by the sunrays; however, the brightness did not cause me to wither. I breathlessly whispered inside,

"Oh' something is budding within this illumination!"
I chortled in my joy. I did not want to leave this luminosity. My full reflection could be seen as I beheld more of my countenance. I stared intently at the glimmering for it was all over my face. My self-talk confidently declared,

"I do not have to leave this place of illumination, for I know I am in the Father and the Father is in me."
I pushed my office chair back with vitality. A slight push from my hand and a swivel in my chair caused me to spin a complete three-hundred and sixty degrees within the glow.

My nature. My disposition. My emotions. My sentiments. My hands. My eyes. My ears. My breast all appeared like dust particles spinning in the sun.

My Spirit now freely turned as the chair revolved in slow and deliberate motion within the rays of truth.

Once the turn-around was complete I grabbed my keys and my purse. I turned the knob to my front door and lightly skipped to my car. I turned the ignition and began my travels to a local Trader Joe's. I stayed in continual praise as I bobbed my head and tried to stay on beat to Yolanda Adams, "It's Already Alright." I would occasionally glance into the rearview mirror.

The glow remained.

I arrived at my local store and every step down the aisles felt as if they were ordered. My attitude of victimization changed. I treaded on my defeat as I stretched my left arm where my lymph nodes continued to swell and grabbed kale, spinach, brussel sprouts, asparagus, squash, pineapples, grapes, apples, bananas, mandarin oranges, broccoli, cauliflower, and tons of water. I reached the juice aisle and it was a pretty difficult task to find a juice without tons of sugar. I eventually grabbed a 100% pineapple juice and headed out of the store.

Of course after paying for my items. I tried to use my glow at the register, but it did not work.

Once home I explained my experience to Anthony and we organized the food into containers and meals for me to eat seven times per day. Fruit was prepared and my herbs and vitamins organized according to the time. Maitake Mushroom, Chlorella, Selenium, Turmeric, Vitamin D, Vitamin C and a good liquid vitamin. After everything was washed and prepared, Anthony looked at me, eye to eye this time and we smiled. In his smile I sensed he felt empowered and now felt his own helplessness being addressed. His prayers were now being answered.

The next morning my 3:00 a.m. time arrived and I joyfully walked to my office. I turned to sit at my desk and I notice a bottle of water, a bowl of grapes, banana's, apples, and oranges. Internally I smiled for Anthony and I both understood we were headed in the right direction and we were in agreement. I ate and continued in Genesis; the story of Noah, Abraham, Enoch and Seth. I desired to process the stories until it was time for my vitamins and then my second meal. The aroma of spinach and broccoli was in the air, I walked in the kitchen and my next meal was ready. I thanked Anthony and headed back to my office and continued my reading.

In the background I still received numerous calls with healing scriptures and offers to get me to Benny Hinn's next meeting. I opened myself to the comments, fears, biases, hopes and patterns of responses of others and I began to formulate more questions. I listened to everyone's responses and their questions were revealing destructive patterns.

However, my level of comprehension was growing beyond the physical limitations of my eyes and ears; my roots were mounting in beneficial soil. I refused to allow my buds to be plucked.

Hearing the voice with me constantly, I was always

reminded, "this need to see this." I invited the group to join in with me for 3:00 a.m. prayer daily.

I shared the Living word that was now my life force. I shared my new lifestyle. We organized times for us to pray collectively. We would meet at a designated home a few times throughout the process. I knew collectively everyone would not roll out of their bed at 3:00 a.m., but I was very aware of the ones who fell to their knees at 3:00 a.m. to continue to search his face and agree with what we understood as truth over the situation.

Our first collective meeting was amazing, my family poured in from the youngest to the eldest and we laid out all over my mother's floors throughout her home. Some completely face down in a prone prostrate before the Lord. Some on their knees and some stood in his presence. I continually expressed the word and information I received and our actions had to line up with the living word. My belief and understanding of truth expressed and now let us touch and agree. I could not waiver, nor allow any bias to alter the revelation I was receiving. Tons of veggies, fruits and water poured into our home continually.

I stood right where I felt God wanted me to stand after seeking his face first for myself.

Several people would continue in their "curse without cause would not come" speeches. I would kindly give them their leash back to place around their own necks…by expressing my understanding of,

"Can any hide himself in secret places that I shall not see him? Do not I fill the heaven and earth?"

I was coming to know God was fully aware of who I was at that time and the choices I made. I knew if I continued to stay in his face, God, work on my understanding to address all the choices I made in my misunderstanding.

Once I shinned light on the dark area, the comments would temporarily stop.

The house of cards I was living in my physical world still felt very uncomfortable; an unfamiliar dwelling in my life anchored by a large, deadly mass in my body and a shattered sense of safety in our world system.

As, I continued to look at the incongruities becoming visible right before my eyes. My judgement was sharpening and discernment was piercing through my hiding spaces.

I could now see my favorite hide-a-way in the corner of my closet, it was narrow enough for me to sit with my knees pulled into my chest and still remain in the shadows. Although the door would open, the light would make a perfect V-shape.

The light would stop right before it reached my skin. In this closet the common wardrobe was missing and in the place of clothing, scriptures were hanging from the ceiling to the floor.

There I would sit clutching my knees into my chest as I attempted to hide behind the word of God, believing this would prevent exposure.

In this place of new revelation, I could see myself as the anomaly. Everyone around me appeared very similar as their actions displayed their true make-up, revealing the hiding closets we walked around carrying.

Beginning to see through the actions of others and more importantly myself. We knew how to dress for church, knew when to say 'Amen' and studied the scriptures by quoting and regurgitating the word; however, how much of it was becoming digested? Digested and then used on cellular levels to become part of our physical make-up. Daily errors and unwillingness to let go of our erring beliefs were being revealed. In my conversations and intimate times of stillness it became clear:

"God, it is easier to continue to say what will happen as a result of sin, instead of focusing on the results of truth. For to seek truth and to walk in understanding would require a vexatious bareness to see my life in totality and to truly see my image…even the areas I attempt to hide in that closet."

I thought of all the times I heard from cheating spouses or
addicts, "It's a family curse." How accommodating the
knowledge of the curse became instead of seeking truth. Truth
would require accountability. Hummm... "to whom much is
given, much is required. Blessed and cursed are opposing
forces. One or the Other."

The wheels of life would keep moving.

There I was driving at a busy intersection. From where I was
driving the light was yellow and all matter around was moving
in a slow motion. The cars parallel to me and the cars driving in
opposition were driving slowly enough for me to see. I was able
to read their license plates: tradition, redundancy, fear, erring
beliefs and biases. I looked to my right and the world system
filled with the almighty dollar was at the stop light in a blue car.

Directly in front of me was the car labeled cancer. I sat in
my transparent car and my personalized plates said, 'learn your
image'. I continued driving in the middle watching all the
locomotion. Ironically, cancer just appeared like one of the
other cars on this highway; all the same compact size and
oblong shape.

I continued to drive in my car glancing briefly at the cars
driving parallel. My own personal car and the direction we
were going was of my main concern. But where were we
going?

Staying on the right lane would get me to my destination; concentrating on one of the other cars on the road would slow my progress. I smiled as I glanced through my window at the cars I passed with great unstoppable force; progression was happening on the wheels labeled awakening.

As quickly as I acknowledged this, the voice spoke, "Read Job."

"What was established in Job...hum, what was established in Job?" I wondered.

I hushed the background noise and continued eating seven times per day, 3:00 a.m. praise, worship and then silence continued daily. The gentle voice within would remind me to be still and stay right there. My ability to answer or dissect between the noises became easier for truth was becoming my sharp sickle.

My vision continued to change. I was no longer seeing the world with my natural eyes; my spiritual eyes were losing their blur.

The voice of truth was with me constantly. My steadiness and diet propelled me to an unbelievable place of understanding. Truth was ever present. I worshipped in spirit and in truth. My erring beliefs were being torn down and my identity was becoming visible.

The bareness was welcomed. I understood God already knew every scar, blemish and wound. As my spirit recognized its own face in the mirror. Past choices, misunderstandings and scars were just seen as dust particles and as the water continued to fill my spiritual man; the dust became like moldable clay. Transformation was becoming visible in my physical world.

One afternoon I was sitting and reading something on the internet and a news flash announced:

"MARVIN SAPP's WIFE HAS DIED FROM CANCER!"

My God, this news hit me pretty hard.

I had to ask myself a difficult question,

> "God, I know she had thousands praying for her ...God why? God, why are we not seeing more manifestation?"

Before I could sit with my question, my phone ...

RING, RING, RING.

My mother was on the other end. I answered and immediately I could sense her fear, I did not know how, but I could feel a paralyzing fear. I listened as her meditations took shape as she asked,

"What did the doctor say? What did the doctor say?" The dots circled around me and connected in front of my eyes.

"My God, my mom can quote the bible back and forth. Scripture by scripture, verse by verse. Her thirty minute prayers sound as if they were full of authority; but here she is asking me what the doctor said about my health and she asks this question every time she calls"

We have been in corporate prayer and individual prayer and she is asking me, "What did the doctor say?" I gently responded,

"What do you believe?"

My question did not bring her comfort, nor did it start an introspective process.

My unwillingness to answer her question left a span in time as I allowed her thoughts to fill in the void. In the void her thoughts, biases and dread spoke as she assumed the worst. She ended our conversation with and auto-pilot response, "Walk by faith."
Amused at the contradiction and saddened concurrently, for she was unaware of her contradiction in behavior. I informed her,

"I will no longer answer that question. For the doctors do not have final say. Their word is not authority."

Straightaway, my knowledge of Job now manifested in my speech. I did not have to memorize it, nor write in on an index card, I declared it.

"Hear diligently my speech and my DECLARATION with your ears. Behold now, I have ordered my cause. Thou shalt decree a thing and it shall be established unto thee; and the light shall shine upon your ways."

The noise on the phone became transparent, for I knew truth was established. I politely left the phone conversation.

The veils I studied in prayer were taking shape. I could see the cloaks. The inward process of acknowledging my own self-placed barriers began.

During one of my prayer times, I sat with index cards preparing myself to learn the scriptures. My patterns of redundancy and mimicking what was done before me played like a comic strip. I knew the word was drawing me deeper and I could not get there by doing redundant patterns without understanding. I ripped my index cards up and allowed the living word to simply become alive.

Seven times per day I ate, 3:00 a.m. I started with praise, worship and then silence. Every day, consistently and consecutively; I did not miss a day.

Once I stopped eating from everyone's table my clarity was absolutely magnificent. The revelations were breath taking and I no longer craved food by man. My hunger continued to grow and I wanted more of this place. The voice was always clear now.

The scriptures continued to take shape; to pop off the pages and become alive. The book that once never made sense and was full of contradictions, mythical beings and parabolic language, suddenly danced in front of me like they were on stage. I could touch the energy and power as the words danced near my nose. As my face drew nearer to the words I began to see myself in the stories of Jacob, Noah, Moses, David and Jesus.

I pictured myself moving through the words, the stories and the parables. Slowly I licked my lips and the sweet taste was always present.

As I continued to observe the electricity striking through the words as they became alive right before my eyes; understanding of the spiritual meaning of the stories popped out like a pop book. My longing to know his face could not be quenched, I held on to my questions as I read....

3:00 a.m., I smiled as I turned to my clock. I attempted to get my suggested ten hours of rest per day, but I absolutely loved this part of my day. I would sit on the edge of my bed and grab a towel that I now kept near to wipe the sweat that was evidence of my immune system trying to work throughout the night. Determined, I pulled my drenched hair back from sticking to my face. I quietly walked down my dim and quiet hallway. I reached my stairs, with my office in my eyes view. I did not peek in on my attachments to this world, for everything in this world belongs to Him. I reached my office. I turned my light on full blast. I turned my praise music on as loud as I could without waking up the entire house. I clapped my hands to the sounds of worship.

My head bounced to the drums as I could feel the rhythm in synch with my heart. Material items in the office one-by-one disappeared as my shouts of worship became a force that broke through physical matter.

My words were filled with energy. Nothing could stop the force (understanding) behind my words. I shouted and ascended both arms, no longer in defiance to the tumor. The tumor was just a name and I was in the presence of the name Above all Names. My statement was clear as I outstretched my arms and worshiped in spirit and in truth.

Truth was becoming visible. My faith was becoming evident. As soon as I acknowledge that fact, my thoughts were quickly interrupted by a mob of people. The mob all spoke at the same time:

"Faith, Hope, Believe! Keep The Faith! Walk by Faith. Faith, Girl! Faith over Fear! Faith! Faith! Faith! Faith! Faith!"

I listened to the statements and they were derived from Scripture; however, did they possess understanding?

"Okay God, what are you showing me?"

Clearly, I heard:

"Read where I tell you to read. Every time you see the word faith, substitute the word 'faith' for the Statement, 'your understanding of truth'"

Learning to follow the voice. I read as I was instructed:

- "For we walk by 'understanding of truth' and not by Sight.
- Woman thy 'understanding of truth hath made you whole.

- Through 'understanding of truth we know the worlds were framed by the word of God, so that things which are seen, were not made of things which do appear.
- Without 'understanding of truth, it is impossible to please him; for he that comes to God must believe that he is a rewarder of those that diligently seek him
- Verily, I say unto you, if you have 'understanding of truth, and doubt not, ye shall do this which is done to the fig tree, but also if ye shall say unto this mountain Be thou removed and be thou cast into the see; it shall be done.
- By 'understanding of truth' the walls of Jericho fell down.
- For by 'understanding of truth' we stand."

The pins that held my world together jingled making the sounds of keys. My globe shifted and my worldview changed. Fully aware of a paradigm shift, the philosophy of my life reformed.

Emunah-faith: truth, firmness, honesty, steadiness. The first representation I could find while studying Emunah was seen in the battle between the Israelites and Amalekites. *(Listen)*

In absolute awe, I studied until I fell asleep. Man, I had to fall asleep. I could not believe I would ever reach a place where the word was actually making sense and I longed to read more. I did not want to stop. I felt He longed to give me understanding.

YEEEEEESSSSSSSSSSSSSSSSSS!

I danced in this place of awakening. For he turned my mourning into dancing.

I twirled with my dance partner as we dipped and spun in the rhythm of revelation. We ballroom danced in this place as the fullness of joy twirled near us. Jehovah Rophe lightly feather stepped around the glow. Jehovah Nissi, Jehovah Jireh, and other attributes of my understanding freely spun around in the very energy of my spoken words.

As we continued to dance we held each other close and in one swift ball change dance move there was a syncopated feeling present. Willingly, I released my weight against my partner; strengths became weak and weaknesses became strong.

As I remained in this leaning position against my partner, Jehovah Nissi twirled in very close to my skin. Jehovah Jireh, Jehovah Rophe and other attributes of my understanding danced until stopping near my outward man. They stopped.

I twirled one more time and the line of demarcation was blurred. I could no longer see where the brightness of their light began and where my understanding ended. Slowly my partner pulled my arm up high and with His hand He spun me and in one complete three- hundred and sixty degree turn. My body spun in the vortex of energy created by my understanding.

Little by little, the line or veil was no longer visible. As the dance ended and my partners were no longer visible on the outside. I knew the brightness of my partners were still present. I declared, "The kingdom of God is within me!"

The tears gushed as understanding and wisdom kissed softly as the voice inside whispered;

> "I can never leave you nor forsake you. For the
> kingdom of God is within."

The harmony now flourishing in my worship enhanced the power of our dance. We put on a show in the light and a whole host of witnesses clapped as I danced the 'First Dance' with my Heavenly Father.

In the glow, I wondered what the view from the outside appeared like to others,

"Could all the light shining from this little downstairs room, on this cul-de-sac from the house on the corner be seen?"

I asked myself as I now thought of my brothers and sisters asleep in the darkness. In this place of time very near sunrise; albeit, darkness was still visible. I kept my eyes on the sun.

I smiled as understanding overshadowed me and the brightness made my skin impossible to behold. Once I noticed the glow, I knew where I was headed next in scripture.

Moses began to play like a hologram near my eyes and nose. The intensity of the images caused me to stick my face in closer. I knew I was no longer on the outside looking in, for I was inside. I was inside! The word was alive.

The life of Moses became theatrical. Moses came down from Mount Sinai and when he came down from the mount I looked upon his face and there was just a bright light. Light, light, and more light. I turned and I could see the children of Israel become afraid and in order for the children of Israel to understand, Moses put a veil upon his face.

Moses went back before God and came out glowing with a marvelous light.

When he came out to speak with the children of Israel, Moses put the veil back on. Moses without the veil when he was in God's presence and placing the veil back on to speak to the Children of Israel. This place looped before me and then looped again. My questioning and vision rear-ended as I blurted out,

"Moses took the veil on and off, before the veil was rent from top to bottom!"

The neurons and axons in my brain were popping like firecrackers as revelation tipped my nose.

"Veils, veils, veils!"

Somehow the knowledge surpassed the neurons in my brain and in the dwelling of two planes there was an explosion. I stuttered my interpretation,

"Veil is my outward man…The veil is my outward man! The flesh is the veil. The veil is flesh."

As soon as I blurted my understanding my readings and understanding of Genesis begin to pour from my mouth like water:

"God you were done in Genesis 1 and there was no Adam and Eve! Where is Adam and Eve? You said you were finished and there was no Adam and Eve? You were done! You were done!

And God said, let us make man in our image, after our likeness: and let them have dominion over the fish of the sea, and over the fowl of the air, and over

the cattle, and over all the earth, and over every
creeping thing that creepeth upon the earth. So God
created man in his own image, in the image of God
created he him; male and female and then you rested."
In the middle of creation, I watched as the words
became alive and took shape. As I continued to focus on
scripture, there was a noise in the background, the noise
began to build and grew in intensity. Vociferously, the
sounds of hammers could be heard. Boisterously, sound
attempted to gain my attention. The piercing sound of glass
caused me turn my head to look at my office walls. I looked
upon the walls of my office and I could see mirrors, mirrors
and more mirrors. Glass was all around me. I turned back to
scripture and then I turned and took a good look at what was
manifesting in my physical world.

Then mirrors began to turn and spin in
rapid motion in an attempt to gain my attention. I continued
to express my revelation of Genesis in relation to the veil.
I repeated:

"So God created man in his own image, in the image of
God created he him; male and female created he them.
There was no Adam and Eve mentioned at that time."
I continued to say the scripture and instantly I could see
myself sitting at a well. I stared intently at the water.
I looked down into the well and then turned back in my

physical world to look at the mirrors.

The water became like a statue, no movement was seen, as I repeated,

> "So God created man in his own image, in the image of God created he him. There was no Adam and Eve."

I looked into the water and in the stillness and once the water became still, I could see my reflection. I stood up and a full-length mirror formed. I touched my face and eyes while looking in the mirror, my understanding was fully present as my mouth expressed:

> "BUT WE ALL, WITH OPEN FACE BEHOLDING AS IN A GLASS THE GLORY OF THE LORD, ARE CHANGED INTO THE SAME IMAGE FROM GLORY TO GLORY, EVEN AS BY THE SPIRIT OF THE LORD."

My God you are showing me how you view me. How you designed me originally. I touched my new identity as it glowed and I-I continuously wanted more as I asked,

> "God, why Adam and Eve?"

I knew at this intersection, he enjoyed my questions and my hunger. My rhapsodic dialogue continued and I was abruptly interrupted-

"Wrong question, Wrong question! Wrong Question!"

This now felt like a game show and excitement was building up between both parties, I knew I was close to the answer and he laughingly enjoyed my desire to know. I mentally traveled through my children's ministry lessons and Christian school curriculum, where Adam and Eve were always taught as our beginning.

Yes, I could see Adam and Eve as the beginning of man but we were spirit first.

Yes, I have always heard in church to Walk in the Spirit. Walk by the Spirit. However, this revelation was showing me something different, somehow the knowledge that I am spirit first continued to flash before me as I pondered on the beginning. I knew my power existed in that original state; My Heavenly Father was inviting me to know myself as I had always been known to him. I was learning to see myself in my true image.

Every inch of me was enchanted as I now longed for this place of enlightenment;

"Make me understand thy precepts as I meditate on your living words."

Deep meditation and allowing the silence,

"There was no Adam and Eve. He was finished and no Adam and Eve. We are spirit first, we are spirit first."

I continued to enter a place of magnificent light,

"God, why Adam and Eve?"

Clearly, I heard a response.

"Don't ask why, but how? But how? But how? Don't

Ask Why? But How."

I tussled with everything I was taught in my youth. I struggled to let go of the harness of misunderstanding I held on to the harness, because the teachings were part of my physical schema. The teachings once held my world together; how can I let go of the hold? The information my Heavenly Father wanted me to see stuck out like a word search. In the scramble of letters, the words began to connect.

My understanding of Genesis continued to pour out of my mouth with ease, "You are showing me how to manifest matter into this world...not why, but how. You are showing me my true image and the place wherein my power lies (in my original image)." My God, finally I knew at this point we were talking about how to manifest anything into my physical world.

To walk in power, I had to see my true identity. The veil was torn from top to bottom, placing me back in oneness with my creator. In his image he made me, yes I am made in the image of God. If my Heavenly Father indeed is above all, so was I. The separation between My Heavenly Father and myself diminished and the middle partition I erected was torn down. Although it was torn down at the crucifixion...I erected it with my lack of misunderstanding and distorted identity. I kept the partition up. Laughingly, I spoke from my understanding and not memory,

"For I am persuaded, that neither death, nor life, nor angels, nor principalities, nor powers, nor things present, nor things to come, Nor height, nor depth, nor any other creature, shall be able to separate us from the love of God, which is in Christ Jesus our Lord."

The full comprehension I was gaining caused me to label the veil as flesh. I also recalled back in Genesis, after Adam and Eve sinned, God asked them,

"Who told you, you were naked?"

Adam and Eve had no knowledge of the veil, flesh or separation for they walked in the garden with God in proper hierarchy of spirit and flesh. Once I acknowledge this, the Holy Spirit spoke:

" NOW, STUDY THE LIFE OF JESUS."

"By a new and living way, which he hath consecrated for us, through the veil that is to say, his flesh;

But even unto this day, when Moses is read, the veil is upon their heart."

Through the veil, that is to say his flesh. Through the veil that is to say his flesh. I was lead to Hebrews after connecting the pieces, "By a new and living way, which he hath consecrated for us, through the veil, that is to say, his flesh" and next I was lead to Corinthians,

"But their minds were blinded: for until this day remaineth the same veil untaken away in the reading of the testament; but even unto this day, when Moses is read, the veil is upon their heart. Nevertheless when it shall turn to the Lord, the veil shall be taken away."

In continuation of thought in that scripture in Corinthians… "but we all, with open face beholding in a glass the glory of the Lord, are changed into the same image from glory to glory, even as by the Spirit of the Lord.

The skies were opened and the roof ripped off my home. A marvelous light and fresh air was present. Once I crossed that level of understanding the revelations would not stop. I reached a point of no return.

There was no going back. My process over the last couple of weeks, I could clearly see my growth and I could now see the scripture as my true mirror. The more I studied, the more I was opening my eyes to see my true identity.

My genesis was unveiled.
This great and moving force could not be stopped.

The harvest is now, thrust in your sickle and reap. I was told to study Revelations after the studying the life of Jesus.

Everyone around me continued to express their sin-consciousness and I continued to walk in truth and true repentance, which simply means a 'mind shift'. Truth was manifesting.

On a bright and sunny morning, Anthony and I headed to my doctor's appointment. I was greeted by my Oncologist in the waiting area, as we walked to the exam room we laughed and talked about sports and all of his pictures as we walked down a long hallway. The pictures were of the doctor's kids and their college and high school days. I began to share with him stories of my boys and my upcoming wedding to Anthony in Jamaica. As, I continued expressing some of the intimate details of my life, the doctor stopped me:

> "Allissen the morbidity is very high with this form of breast cancer and you are already in a late stage. I don't think you should continue to plan for your wedding.
>
> Your immune system will be so wiped out, attempting to travel will be very dangerous for you. Just enjoy the next six months, a year or two."

His face remained serious and solemn as if he had seen this Time after Time. I understood he was speaking from his Experience and his understanding of truth, so I allowed him to finish his spill. Once he was done, I spoke from my truth. I looked into his eyes and the words poured from my understanding with ease as I simply asked,

> "Can you tell me the number of hairs I have on my head?"

His eyes were enlarged and he looked perplexed.
His facial expression looked as if he wanted to say,

"Did you hear what I just told you and you are talking about hair!"

I did not allow his expressions to move me, I waited on an answer, so I confidently repeated;

"Do you know the number of hairs I have on my head? Do-You-Know-The-Number-of-Hairs-I Have?"

The sound of a 9.8 earthquake rumbled from the spiritual into the physical. Walls were crumbling down and the room vibrated with life; the energy caught the doctor's attention as he stuttered,

"I -I-I do n-ot know the exact number, but, but the average human has …"

I did not give him room to finish.

The words exploded through the clarity now seen through the illuminated area of my reflection. The truth and understanding that renewed my mind was now evident as the outer portion of my mind spoke:

"The very hairs on my head, He knows the number and only He can number my days. I will see you on the next appointment."

The walls completely down to dust. The veil shattered to pieces.

From within I could hear, My Heavenly Father as he spoke…

"Now you recognize the authority you have in you. Now you are walking in my creative power. The same understanding of truth that spoke this world into existence, you now understand! "CALLETH THOSE THINGS WHICH BE NOT AS THOUGH THEY WERE."

My legs buckled as I walked in my new freedom without the chains that bound me. I trembled as I walked out of the office and down the same long hallway.

As I walked this hallway and looked at the same frames… I could now see my family in those pictures. I could see my son graduating high school. My baby's first birthday party. I could see my wedding in three months. I could see the images now. I could see it beyond my physical eyes. I walked that hallway to the end and at the end I turned a corner. I turned a corner.

As I turned the corner the tears were streaming as I poured my love on my Heavenly Father. I did not care who could see the tears in the physical, for beyond the veil that once covered my heart, I was loving on My Heavenly Father. Every step I took, I felt as if the word took shape starting with my toes and up my legs, circling around my belly, and beating within my heart. My understanding of the word was tangible and was now a life force. I reached the waiting room and Anthony saw my glow and my trembles.

Through my trembles I was able to express,

"It is finished! It is over! It was finished a many years ago!

Worship, praise and prayer took on a whole new meaning. The clarity is something very difficult for me to describe. I continued with veggies, water, eating seven times per day and beginning prayer at 3:00 a.m.

One morning, I was spread out on my floor in deep worship. Pushing pass this realm came with more ease now, once I recognized my identity.

I opened my eyes during worship one glorious day and I could see my office floor. I opened my eyes during worship and I was looking at my office floor. Everything in my office looked the same, except I could see someone spread out on the floor. I blinked my eyes to make sure I was seeing what I was seeing and I recognized the person on the floor was me.

"Wait a minute, I am above my body." I was above my body…I was above my body! I desired understanding, so I simply asked, "Show me!" Instantly, I could see myself on the floor writing and writing. I hovered and watched myself from above myself writing.

I watched myself drop a pen and then I closed a book. The cover of the book read, *The Valley of Baca.* I watched this happen a few times and then I said the words aloud,

"The Valley of Baca."

As soon as I stated the words, I was back in my body. I touched my face and arms and tried to slow my breathing down. "What just happened? What happened?"

I scrambled off my belly and grabbed my bible. I did not know what Baca meant, nor had I read a scripture with the word Baca. I knew I was in the presence of My Heavenly Father. I searched and searched and there it was big and as bold as ever…Psalms 84:5-7! I looked up the word Baca and it means weeping. I screamed, shouted and danced around my office, my kitchen and living room. Anthony and my boys ran in to see what was going on and I started to ramble on:

"I was in prayer and then I was over myself. I was over myself and I could see my body with these same clothes on and I was face down on the floor…. but I was not there. I was not there. Well, I was there, but on the ceiling. The real me was looking from the ceiling. My Spirit is the real me and I surpassed my flesh and the partitions I created. To be absent from the body is to be present with the Lord. That is now! That is not just in death! I saw myself writing a book and the book is called The Valley of Baca, it is called The Valley of Baca! I took one more breath and blurted: Blessed is the man whose strength is in thee; in whose heart are the ways of them. Who passing through the valley of Baca make it a well; the rain also filleth the pools. They go from strength to strength, every one of them in Zion appeareth before God in Zion"

Vantage Point

Blessed is the man whose strength is in thee; in whose heart are the ways of them.

Who passing through the valley of Baca make it a well; the rain also filleth the pools.

They go from strength to strength, every one of them in Zion appeareth before God.

Psalms 84; 5-7

Their facial expressions were priceless, even the baby looked at me like, "you need a nap." I laughed a real laugh and returned to my office for now I was seeing more purpose and my viewpoint of this trial changed. I was beginning to look at this trial from a different position. Cancer was beginning to look very minuet, next to the bigger picture. Pieces of the larger picture were becoming visible, but I needed more understanding to make the picture work. I now wondered 'why me?' but no longer in a negative way.

"God, what are you showing me to do?" My hunger for understanding continued to increase. I read constantly and just continued to wait as my spirit man continued to erect into proper position. I now welcomed the questions presented to me and I began to develop my own inquiries.

An amazing thing happened, I could to see myself in the center of this trial, and I began to look at it from different angles.

A very common angle that I could see in my first chapter was the "why me" view point."

The second was, "God, just do it over night," my bargaining, crying and pleading viewpoint. The third was full of condemnation, "what did I do to get here? What sin was so horrible?" This fourth viewpoint, which was taking shape right in front of my eyes was empowering and life-changing for it was now based on truth. This vantage point had the ability to clear up misunderstandings and then use true understanding to operate in power.

In this moment I knew this trial was not to take my life, but to transform it and the lives of others.

Quickly, I could see the scripture everyone used to remain very conscious of sin and curses; therefore keeping a forced place veil, but this time I could see it as it were intended to be seen.

"The word of the LORD came unto me again, saying, What mean ye that ye use this proverb concerning the land of Israel, saying, the fathers have eaten sour grapes, and the children's teeth are set on edge?

As I live, saith the Lord GOD, ye shall <u>NOT HAVE *OCCASION* ANY MORE</u> to use this proverb in Israel."

I understood condemnation clearer. The ability to declare yourself guilty without a trial. My ponderings or actions in the beginning of this trial searched for natural understanding. My human and lower level of understanding needed to know cause and effect. I began to really explore my life as the examination process continued in a healthy way.

In the beginning the conflicting thoughts in my mind would always say, God, I believe you can heal me; however, I did such and such acts years ago. My contradictions were so bold and blatant in my face, but I remained blind in my ignorance. In this place of looking at my life from several different vantage points. I realized how much I was holding on to the baggage of previous experience, disappointments, and flat out heart breaks. My first marriage, my divorce, and my childhood, my religious experiences all still had very real hooks in me, keeping me anchored to repetitive childlike experiences. Oh' the 'children of Israel, I could now see how/why they were called 'children'.

Here I was in the middle of seeing myself as a true son of God and I had to accept that I was a perfectly chiseled cliché with redundant behaviors, actions and responses.

I would frame my redundant actions a different way and expect the result to somehow be different, while the content of my actions remained the same.

In this place of asking the necessary questions, I realized it was important to draw up from my inner-self which was of prime importance and this inner classroom was a critical piece to my true understanding, which was unfolding.

Through my obdurate resistance of my physical man and the elements of this world; somehow, I was beginning to regain my misplaced power. I begin to see and operate in my true nature. False images and perceptions began to roll off like tumbleweeds.

Truth became my rhythm and I faced the light unashamed. My life began to exhibit my union with God. My Genesis was unveiled to me.

My self- indulgence of body and emotions, through understanding of my original design began to gain insight. Emotions and self-indulgence are real, the tumor on my chest was real. The emotions I felt were real forces, but I could see how my distorted vision fueled their power.

Seeing and understanding the truth of my original design allowed me to begin to line things up properly.

In the beginning of examining my life, condemnation had to be addressed. My indulgence on causality continued to allow my flesh/veil to keep its illusion of power. The image making power of the mind played on guilt, shame, fear, and hopelessness.

These thoughts did not remain quiescent; they stimulated new actions and new self-indulgence.

My ceaseless desire to know how I caused this and how in the world this was going to end was kinetic and continued to gain energy and more energy. In my response to this initially, I busied myself endlessly with mind images. Those images created more images and my outward expression was to hide in the corner of my office with my hands over my ears in an attempt to stop the inward chatter.

The walls of condemnation began to shatter like glass and in the fragments I could see all the pieces of glass I refused pluck out as they continued to pin me to my worldview. I held on to the shards. The edges were sharp and cutting deep, but I would not let go. They were all I knew and understood.

"God these memories are mine. This worldview is all I know; although, it caused pain and was full of and field with confusion; it was mine."

Those mind images were a hindrance, then again a place of comfort, only because they were what I knew.

I progressed too far to retreat now. I continued in my routine: prayer, reading, praise, eating seven times per day (mostly veggies) and now writing in my journal labeled, '_The Valley of Baca_'.

"For which is easier to say, thy sins be forgiven of thee or to say arise and walk?"

I laughed as I pictured Jesus hitting me upside my forehead and telling me to read this scripture about 10 times... no for you about twenty times. I loved and welcomed the correction. I read this over and over:

> Son, be of good cheer; thy sins be forgiven thee.
> And, behold, certain of the scribes said within themselves, This *man* blasphemeth.
> And Jesus knowing their thoughts said, Wherefore think ye evil in your hearts?
> FOR WHETHER IS EASIER, TO SAY, *THY* SINS BE FORGIVEN THEE; OR TO SAY, ARISE, AND WALK?
> But that ye may know that the Son of man hath power on earth to forgive sins, (then saith he to the sick of the palsy,) Arise, take up thy bed, and go unto thine house.

As I read it for the twentieth time, several important images begin to stick out. First, I understood Jesus knew what our hindrances would be and how much power we would give guilt and sin in our lives to the point of determining, healing or no healing. Success versus failure. IN Him or forever separated.

He is waiting on us to view ourselves in our true image, as the sons of GOD.

Phase 3:

Manifestation

An event, action, or object that clearly shows or embodies something, especially a theory or an abstract idea.

But have renounced the hidden things of dishonesty, not walking in craftiness, nor handling the word of God deceitfully; but by manifestation of the truth commending ourselves to every man's conscience in the sight of God.

For I reckon that the sufferings of this present time _are_ not worthy _to be compared_ with the glory which shall be revealed in us.

For the earnest expectation of the creature waiteth for the manifestation of the sons of God.

For whom he did foreknow, he also did predestinate _to be_ conformed to the image of his Son, that he might be the firstborn among many brethren.

Moreover whom he did predestinate, them he also called: and whom he called, them he also justified: and whom he justified, them he also glorified.

I now see the God that sees me

"Did you see Jelani take a step?" I asked Anthony. He smiled as he answered, "Yes, I saw him." "What do you think about purple and orange for our wedding colors?" "How many people do you think are going to join us at our wedding in Jamaica?"

During our ride to have my full body MRI, we talked about normal aspects of our world as Anthony's eyes sparkled. I looked at him intently beyond my natural eyes and images began to flash before me. In the images I could feel how helpless he felt over the last couple of weeks.

The image took me deeper and further beyond the last couple of weeks, actually the images took me to years prior. I could see him in his childhood. In the image he looked around twelve or thirteen, he was in a car and I could feel his emotions and once again I could sense he felt completely helpless.

I looked at him driving, while looking at a parallel image of him in his youth. I continued to look at the young Anthony and suddenly I heard:

"I need him to know that I am real and I was there; he needs to fully believe again for where I am taking him."

I did not hesitate to verbalize the images flashing before me, Anthony pulled over to the side of the street. Tears were welling in his eyes as he explained more details of his father's death from multiple myeloma:

"You know Allissen, my mom and I left Coldwell Elementary and we were driving and we reached Florence Boulevard in Los Angeles. An ambulance crossed the intersection and I said, 'Mom, follow that ambulance.' My mom followed that ambulance. I knew my dad was in that Ambulance. I knew that would be the last time I had with my dad. The ambulance pulled into Daniel Freeman Hospital and we pulled in behind it. We got out and there was my dad in the back of that ambulance. They rolled him in and I got up close, very close to see him.

He looked to find me. He found me and he smiled. He smiled and then he died right in that moment. They resuscitated him one time while driving and then he saw me and died."

I explained to him that I could not see everything that was going on in the car, but I felt the emotions in the car.

Helplessness, helplessness and more helplessness all around the car; the emotions felt was helplessness and somehow God wants to speak with you through this situation to address that barrier.

I noticed a tear drop from his eyes. I closed my mouth. I decided to leave room in the silence for his inner voice to speak. We made it home and I ate my veggies and fruit and threw in a load of laundry. I opened my windows and allowed the breeze to circulate the lemongrass scent throughout our home. I grabbed a glass of water and sat in my office to study.

We scheduled a full-body MRI finally and it was scheduled for a week away. My entire body would be scanned at that time. I continued in deep prayer, meditation and eating seven times per day. Revelations and new abilities continued to make themselves known to me.

During this time my son played basketball and I attended most of his games and while at one game a woman passed by me and as she passed by, I heard, "She has breast cancer."

It was loud and clear. I looked at Anthony and my son and I blurted out, "she is going through something." Anthony and my son looked at me, like what are you talking about. I could not explain what I heard, but I knew I heard it. This was a new experience and I did not know what to do, so I walked away and did not speak to her. "God, what was I supposed to say?" My son would later come to me asking for a pink ribbon for his uniform, because his friend's mom passed from breast cancer. It was the same lady.

My inability to trust what I heard for a stranger bothered me and I took it to God in prayer and I apologized for missing it and I would not allow that to happen again. I pushed passed my error and continued in praise, worship, and the stillness.

Full body MRI day! The wind blew forcefully, but the sun shinned bright, while we walked on the grounds of City of Hope.

I looked at Anthony as he walked another direction. I noticed on my shirt there were water drops. I touched my face and tears were running down.

My God, these tears are not my own and once I acknowledged the tears… I could hear the lamentations of several people. I yelled out to Anthony, "Do you hear that? These are not my tears; do you hear that?" He was too far away to hear me. I continued to walk towards the hospital section and the voices became clearer as they stated,

"God, why are you doing this to me? Why? Why? Why?"

The anguish accompanied with the voices caused me to sit down.

"God, I said I would never miss it again, but what am I supposed to do here?"

I could not shake the emotions of the others and suddenly I heard a gentle voice,

"They are attracted to your light!"

I quickly responded,

"My light! This is too much, how do I push them away?"

No answer this time. I ran into the chapel located at the hospital as I waited on my MRI. I am about to have a full body scan to see if my body is full of cancer, this is not the day for a new experience. The voices and cries would not leave me as I sat in the waiting area. My legs bounced up and down until the technician called me in for my MRI.

I hesitantly walked into the room and the technician could read my body language and asked, "Do you need an Ativan?" I quickly responded, "No, I will be okay," I laid chest down on the table and allowed my breast to rest in the area of the table. The machine began to circle around and around with such a loud noise.

The noise of the people and the machine was overwhelming and the disharmony caused a clash in my bones. "Pull me out, Please!"

The technician quickly entered the room and stopped the machine. I could not explain with words what I heard and felt. I felt if I did express it, I might be sent to the psych unit. I staggered my words to the technician as the tears poured.

All I could tell the technician, "These are not my feelings!" She pulled up a chair near the machine and held my hand. Slowly the table slid back into the machine and the noise began. Around and around, clank, clank, clank!

Surrounded by noise, but I closed my eyes and took deep breaths. I kept the mirror with me always now; I closed my eyes and took a good look. In my mind, I began with praise and worship and then silence. The voices slowly silenced and the circles of the MRI machine moved slow, then slower.

The swirls of the machine went slower and slower until

they stopped. The loud machine stopped. The noises stopped.

I opened my eyes and I was looking at myself as a girl around the age of 12 or 13, I was sitting on the floor watching television.

Once again I am on the ceiling. I was on the ceiling looking at a younger version of myself. Suddenly, I heard a large slam against the wall. I looked to the right as I heard my cousin scream. Next, I could hear, "Bitch this and Bitch that!" I attempted to turn my head as I watched from above, "God why are you showing me this?" I turned back as I heard another scream, when I looked back he was dragging her up the stairs. I turned away for I could still feel the emotions I felt as that thirteen-year-old child. I shouted,

"Call the police!"

I turned to grab the phone and I thought about calling the police, but I felt they would take too long to get there. I grabbed the phone to call my grandmother, oh', but she did not drive. I paced back and forth thinking what to do. I was too small and unable to fight off the monster. I could hear glass breaking and doors slamming. I walked closer to the stairs and I took two steps up and out of fear I quickly ran down.

"God why are you showing me this? I don't want to live this again?"

I looked back down and I saw my younger self standing at the stairs again. My heart was racing through my chest and no help was coming for her; except me, but what was I going to do? I paced from the steps to the kitchen.

The fighting continued and I heard one more loud glass shatter. I ran back to the stairs. I passed the first step. I passed the second step. Once I reached the second step, I heard another glass break and one more scream.

Once the glass broke something in me also broke. I leaped off that second step and flew over the next five steps. From the ceiling I watched in slow motion.

From the ceiling as I watched myself step out of fear. The most powerful voice spoke:

"MULTIPLY IT! MULTIPLY IT! THE LOVE YOU FELT THEN, MULTIPLY IT! HE THAT DWELLED IN LOVE, DWELT IN GOD, AND MY LOVE IS PERFECTED IN HIM."

I continued to run up the stairs and I hit a long hallway. The hallway was dark and her room was the last door at the end of this hallway. I ran as fast as I could.

My Heavenly Father spoke in his powerful voice;

"Everlasting, Everlasting, Yes, I have loved thee with an everlasting love; therefore, with lovingkindness I have drawn you"

The tears were pouring from my natural eyes and the energy of what was going on above the MRI machine caused my physical body to shake. I continued to watch a younger me take steps of pure love as I rejected my fear.

I burst through my cousin's bedroom door, not knowing what to do; my eyes caught eyes with my cousin as she was attempting to cover her face and her pregnant belly.

I simply laid my body across her body and accepted, if he hit her again, he was going to have to hit me. The powerful voice still spoke as my experience replayed:

"I TOOK YOUR BRUISES. I WAS BRUISED FOR YOUR INIQUITIES."

The powerful voice spoke again and gave me direction to look at the face of the person as he reacted to my actions….Oh' he did not see a thirteen-year-old child. He saw love, love and more love.

The chaos stopped and the tranquility flourished, both in the physical room and in this magnificent light I bathed in above the MRI. Passion and mercy surrounded me. You were always there!

No height, no depths, no sin, and no shame can separate me from your love. Love that knows my name. In this place I knew I became the scripture. I knew his love was poured out at the cross and I could now answer the question,

"For what is easier to say, thy sins be forgiven or to say arise and walk?"

My heart overflowed with joy and it did not matter that I had a 6.7-centimeter, high grade tumor in my chest and all throughout my lymph nodes. Everything I needed was already known and being revealed. For I now understood any veils erected were forced placed by myself. The veil that masked my heart was comprised of shame, fear, guilt, past pain and misunderstandings. Misunderstandings.

The technician pulled me from the MRI machine and still held on to my hand. The technician had tears running down her face; the love and energy I experienced flowed like a force running through my body and all through my hands. Like fire in my bones. I hugged her as I laughed a laugh that was full of freedom.

I did not look beyond the glass to read the other technicians reactions to my scans. In the past I would look to see if they were smiling? Could I get a thumbs up or something? It did not matter this time, for I knew Allissen's name was changed and her identity was now as it was originally designed.

He was waiting on me and has always known me:
For the earnest expectation of the creature waiteth for the manifestation of the sons of God. For whom he did foreknow, he also did predestinate to be conformed to the image of his Son, that he might be the firstborn among many brethren.

The scripture is a mirror in whence I learned my true image.

I ran from the MRI room to the gift shop and I purchased items and wrote notes of love. I found one of the Social Workers and asked her to give the gifts to patients, whom no one visits. On each note I wrote:

"Perfect love cast out all fear and although it may not feel like it, God loves you with an everlasting love and so do I."

My experience in the MRI was life changing and I was never the same. Overall the entire process, God was revealing bits and pieces of areas of my life. I always found myself asking aloud, "You saw that? You were there with that?"

The more being revealed to me the more I understood and I declared, that God was my Heavenly Father and I was his daughter with a purpose. The purpose was bigger than me and could not be revealed, nor completed without God's help and me recognizing, in his image he made me and he was pleased.

My God knew me before the world was formed, the God that saw my childhood and was there in difficult places. The God that was there as I hid in the corner of my office and asked me question after question.

Each question was rhetorical in nature and used to initiate more questions to ask myself. I now could see him in the room with me, I could see his purpose in the questions.

I no longer had to look up in the sky and project my voice; for I could sing right to him. Conversation is the most intimate act and I enjoyed his touch, his face as we communicated with each other. My experiences sitting at the well to look at my reflection was to allow me to see myself as I had always been seen, before the world was formed.

The experience of Hagar became alive and I could see myself at the well called Beerlahairoi; the well of the living one that seeth me. I could now see God as he saw me and I could see the God that see's me. El Roi.

> "and she called the name of the LORD that spake unto her, Thou God sees me: for she said, Have I also here looked after him that seeth me?"

I could now look at the face of the one whom sees me always.

After that day, I would receive numerous calls per day from people constantly needing to talk and looking for direction. They did not care about my physical condition, nor ask; my mother would attempt to intercept the calls. I had to remind her as I heard it,

> "They are attracted to my light.
>
> In him is life and that life is light unto men."

The scripture is a mirror in whence I learned my true image.

Let's Go to the Other Side

"I guess you are going to Jamaica," said my Medical Oncologist as he sat with a bewildered look upon his face. "Your labs are amazing and you do not need to go further, for we can find,"

No Evidence of Disease.

I just laughed for we were flying out in a few weeks. I smiled and gave him a hug, "I will send you some pictures," as I walked out of his office and headed to my final dress fitting.

My Sister-Cousin whom, My Heavenly Father used in the powerful story to remind me of the power of love. She stayed with me a lot throughout my process. My final dress fitting arrived and she was there,

"What do you think about my dress?"

We burst into laughter and only we understood, for our laughter had nothing to do with that dress, for I could care less about the dress.

I was there. I was there.

I was diagnosed with Late Stage III, Her2neu+, high grade tumor with lymph node involvement on February 19, 2009. The tumor was 6.7 cm and several lymph nodes were involved. At that time, women diagnosed with my stage and aggressiveness statistically 85% were dead within two years.

In April of 2009, (two months later) my doctor's would attempt to have labs redone for they could not understand my progress.

By May (close to June) of that year, (3 months later) I stood in the kitchen opening the refrigerator and I asked my son to touch my chest. For God showed me that he needed my son to see this, when he touched my chest his eyes grew large as he blurted,

"I don't feel anything!"

I smiled as I blurted, "That's right, because it is not there!

In a matter of three months, the doctors could find, No Evidence of Disease.

My radiation oncologist from the City of Hope shared with me:

"I have only seen this one other time in my entire career. For the tumor to be completely gone before surgery, I have seen it only in one other woman."

My understanding ears perked and I wanted to meet the ONE other person. I definitely asked, however, because of confidentiality he could not release the information. Every time I am on the grounds of City of Hope, I know I will one day run into her for us to exchange notes.

June 25, 2009, all of our bags packed, passports, and each other. No extra wedding stresses, for they did not matter. Close to forty people would travel with us to Jamaica for our union.

We were ready to go.

My first morning in Jamaica, I was accustomed to waking up for praise and worship very early, so while in Jamaica nothing would change. I opened my eyes in my beautiful room and I heard beautiful sounds coming from outside. The sounds were glorious.

I felt as if the sounds were calling me.
I rolled out of bed and followed the sounds. I walked around on this beautiful resort following the sounds. I reached a large foyer and I could see rows and rows of people. They were lined up on the stairs, hanging over the balconies and standing directly in front of me. Lines and lines of people and they were all in various work uniforms. I stood there in awe as I listened to the sounds they caroled.

A large portion of the staff stood with their arms raised singing praises to God. All of their voices spoke of his goodness, his mercy and his sovereignty.
The sounds, the sounds were so amazing. What Love!

I turned and joined the staff of the resort with tears running down my face. I continued to do what I would normally do to start my morning.

Praise. Worship. Stillness. Praise. Worship. Stillness. Praise. Worship. Stillness. The sounds were so heavenly and in the singing I heard;

> "We were waiting on you to get here. We knew you would get here ...to join in."

June 27, 2009 at sunset. As the sun slowly went down in Jamaica. Our light was still shinning.

The music began (if you have Bob Marley and the Wailers 'Is This Love', turn it up loud...louder. Now read the words:

I want to love you, and treat you right,
I want to love you, every day and every night,
We'll be together, with a roof right over our heads,
We'll share the shelter, of my single bed,
We'll share the same room, yeah! For Jah provide the bread.
Is this love, is this love, is this love,
Is this love that I'm feelin'?
Is this love, is this love, is this love, Is this love that I'm feelin'?
I want to know, want to know, want to know now!
I got to know, got to know, got to know now!
I, I'm willing and able,
So I throw my cards on your table!
I want to love you, I want to love and treat, love and treat you right,
I want to love you every day and every night,
We'll be together, yeah! With a roof right over our heads,
We'll share the shelter, yeah, oh now! of my single bed,
We'll share the same room, yeah
! For Jah provide the bread.
(Is This Love, Bob Marley, 1978).

The saxophonist blew the notes to Bob Marley's song. There was not a dry eye at our wedding. We had people coming up to us for days after our wedding telling us,

"I did not mean to pry, but something was drawing me to your wedding."

The staff would tell us,

"We do a lot of weddings, but something was different about yours."

We danced. We laughed.

One Love!

Jamaica is the birthplace of my husband's natural father. Delano W. Jones.

A black butterfly followed us our entire wedding day. My husband sparkled as he toured the land of his father with his sons. We reached a town that once had no electricity.

My Father-in–law, Delano W. Jones, before he died from multiple myeloma (cancer) used his understanding of electricity to bring light to that little town in Jamaica.

We laughed. We danced, in the light of that city.

Healing.

"As it was in the beginning, so shall it be in the end. There is no hiding place from the Father of Creation." Bob Marley (One Love/Bob Marley, 1978).

The Valley of Baca.

Every one of them in Zion appeareth before God.

Zion: the highest place of Spiritual Awakening.

This one was born in Zion.

Mr. and Mrs. Jones

Allissen C. Jones,
Founded The Just Believe Project, Inc.
There are several projects through our Non-Profit
Corp.
1. **Breast Cancer awareness and Advocacy**
2. **Addressing the Barriers to Believing (Why are we not seeing more manifestation.**
3. **Housing Projects for the terminally ill~ Every moment of life should be lived.**
4. **Let's Go to the Other Side Publishing~ Several books and tools to address barriers.**

Allissen was given this task at a point in her life where in real time all hope appeared to be dissipating in the wind. Allissen is a great example that today does not have to look like yesterday; Yesterday does not have to rule over your tomorrow, nor your years to come... If you face it. Allissen uses her life in a demonstrative way to model her simple concept of addressing the barriers to believing. Through her real-life experiences and education, Allissen attempts to bring awareness of the self-placed barriers that need to be torn down with the knowledge of God. With real understanding.

Allissen possess a Master's in Psychology and is currently working on her Doctorate in Clinical, Psychology. In addition, Allissen is a Licensed Nurse with emphasis in Psychiatric disorders.
Her desire to see real growth, real change in real people is tangible. She has worked at Chino Prison, RJ Donovan Prison, and Centinela State Prison. She has spent years studying behavior, personality disorders and mental illness.

Join us with our Non-profit organization:

The Just Believe Project, Inc.

www.thejustbelieveproject.org

www.thevalleyofbaca.com

Follow us: Allissen and Anthony Jones on Facebook

Like our page and follow for updates and new releases

Email: acjones@thevalleyofbaca.com

For speaking engagements, questions, help, or donations.

References and key scriptures:
King James Bible

Psalms 84; 5-7	Luke 22:46	Sng of Sol. 2:15
Psalms 89:27	I Peter 1:13	Ezekiel 18:2
Psalms 90:10	II Samuel 5:23	Isaiah 5:4
Isaiah 54:17	Jeremiah 23:24	Deut, 8, 3-4
II Corinthians 12:4	Galatians 3:21-22	Exodu34: 27-35
Psalms 108	II Corinthians 13	Isaiah 25:7
Psalms 87:6	II Corinthians 3	II Cor. 3:13
Ezekiel 3:23	Matthew 9:20	Hebrews 6:19
Ezekiel 2	Matthew 9:5	Hebrews 10:20
Psalms 110	Genesis 1 (All)	Rom 8:19
Isaiah 8:18	Romans 11:26	II Cor. 3:18
Joel 3	II Samuel 5, 6-7	
Jeremiah 19:2	Philippians 3, 4-5	
Ezekiel 3:22	II Timothy 2:25	
Genesis 26:19	II Corinthians 6, 16-18	
2 Kings 3:16	I Samuel 12:24	
II Samuel 5:7	John 16;18 & 18:37	
Hebrew 12:22	Proverbs 4	
Isaiah 60:14	Genesis 17, 7-8	
I Peter 2:6	Genesis 26, 3-5	
Genesis 14:18	Jeremiah 31	

WHAT MANNER OF LOVE IS THIS?

His Heart, Her Breast, Their Love; Greater Love.

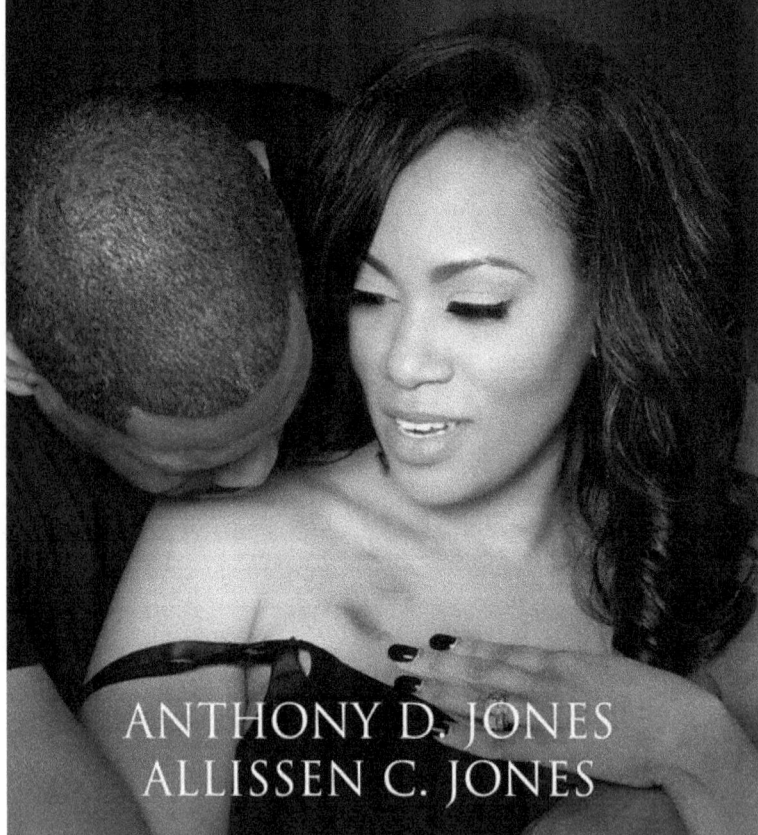

ANTHONY D. JONES
ALLISSEN C. JONES

www.ingramcontent.com/pod-product-compliance
Lightning Source LLC
Chambersburg PA
CBHW052036090426
42739CB00010B/1933